Winning Over Weaknesses

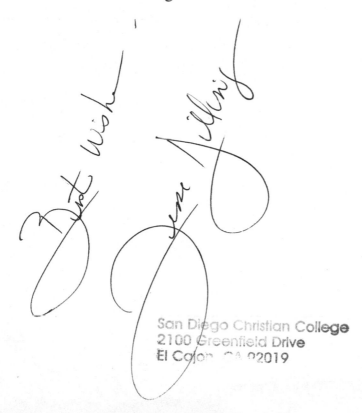

WINNING OVER WEAKNESSES

How to Turn Them Into Strengths

JESSE DILLINGER

SERVANT PUBLICATIONS
ANN ARBOR, MICHIGAN

Vine Books is an imprint of Servant Publications especially designed to serve evangelical Christians.

Servant Publications—Mission Statement
We are dedicated to publishing books that spread the gospel of Jesus Christ, help Christians to live in accordance with that gospel, promote renewal in the church, and bear witness to Christian unity.

Scripture quotations, unless otherwise indicated, are taken from the HOLY BIBLE, NEW INTERNATIONAL VERSION®. Copyright 1973, 1978, 1984 by International Bible Society. Used by permission of Zondervan Publishing House. All rights reserved.

Servant Publications
P.O. Box 8617
Ann Arbor, MI 48107
www.servantpub.com

Cover design: Noah Pudgil Design

03 04 05 06 10 9 8 7 6 5 4 3 2 1

Printed in the United States of America
ISBN 1-56955-354-8

Library of Congress Cataloging-in-Publication Data

Dillinger, Jesse.
  Winning over weaknesses : how to turn them into strengths / Jesse Dillinger.
      p. cm.
Includes index.
  ISBN 1-56955-354-8
  1. Conduct of life. 2. Emotions. 3. Success. I. Title.
  BJ1581.2.D55 2003
  158.1–dc22

                                                          2003013397

Inside every weakness is the substance of strength.
Jesse Dillinger

CONTENTS

Bringing the Very Best Out of Our Very Worst

They will beat their swords into plowshares and their spears into pruning hooks.

ISAIAH 2:4b

Wouldn't it be great not to repeat the same mistakes over and over? Wouldn't it be nice not to repeat to ourselves: "Why did I do that again?" "When will I ever stop doing this?" "Why do I say those things?" Wouldn't it be nice if we weren't plagued by our own weaknesses?

As a marriage and family therapist I've seen many people in despair and pain. They're ashamed of what they've done or who they are. They crumble beneath their weaknesses and the illusion that others don't struggle as they do. Yet we all have weaknesses.

There's something wonderful about weaknesses. If we have the courage to recognize and confront them, they'll become a secret source of great strength. What are these weaknesses? Where do they come from? How are we supposed to handle them? That's what *Winning Over Weaknesses* is all about.

Like the swords and the plowshares in Isaiah 2:4b, our weaknesses are made of the very same substance as our strengths. The weaknesses that could destroy us are the very same things that we can use to become strong and successful. This book is about the process of turning those weaknesses into strengths. It's about taking our worst and making it our best. All weaknesses are gold mines of opportunity. They can give us more understanding of ourselves and others. We can use them to develop strengths of character, compassion, and the right perspective. All of these valuable characteristics and more are at risk of

11

being underdeveloped unless we acknowledge and deal with our weaknesses. In this book I'll help you identify your weaknesses and show you how to turn them into strengths.

It's just a part of being human to have weaknesses. It's not honest to blame our parents or our environments for the way that we think and behave. We think and behave as we do because we choose to. In this book, we'll look to the past in order to determine the origin of our choices, not to blame someone else for them.

Whether our weaknesses are recent developments or childhood acquisitions, it's important to understand them. Wherever possible, it's to our advantage to determine why we've developed these weaknesses, and what purposes they've come to serve in our lives. When we've done that, we can determine whether these purposes still exist today. When we've identified the weaknesses, found their origins, and challenged their purposes, we'll then be prepared to transform these weaknesses into strengths.

At the end of each section dealing with weakness is a portion of the section called *Companion Weaknesses*. The numbers in this section correspond to a list by the same name in the index at the back of the book. This is a list of the weaknesses covered in *Winning Over Weaknesses*. Since weaknesses tend to occur in clusters, I've placed a check mark next to the weaknesses that most commonly accompany the weakness in that section. This will provide you with an idea of how weaknesses tend to be connected.

Although the stories in this book are loosely based on actual accounts, names and details of the stories have been changed to protect privacy.

In this book I won't be dealing with any real or potential genetic, biological, medical, or psychiatric aspects of weaknesses. My book is not a substitute for medical, psychiatric, or psychological treatment. If you need assistance in any of those areas, please consult someone within those professions.

On a Personal Note

I could never write this book from the cool distance of someone untouched by weaknesses. There was a time when I thought that my struggles with my own weaknesses would be the end of me. Yet, dealing with them was, in fact, my beginning. Discovering why I thought the way I did and did the things I did became my road to freedom and success. I know what it's like to have thought and behaved in ways that were destructive to me and to others. Yet, I've learned now how to change those thoughts and behaviors. In fact, I've learned how to turn them into strengths. I can show you how to do that as well.

I've deliberately chosen to use the pronoun "we" throughout this book. As you read *Winning Over Weaknesses,* I want you to know that I'm going along with you. I want you to remember that I was there once, too. I'll show you how weaknesses develop and how to handle them. It's my earnest desire that you find your own way out of the grasp of weaknesses and join me here on the other side, where weaknesses are no longer the norm but occasional experiences from which I still learn and grow.

Throughout this book I'll be suggesting that we live by what I'm calling the current truth. I want to explain what I mean so there's no confusion. I think the Old Testament offers us great wisdom here. For starters, truth isn't relative. It doesn't change. "Truthful lips endure forever, but a lying tongue lasts only a moment" (Prv 12:19).

Principle: Truth is not relative. It doesn't change according to what we want it to be. It's our perception of the truth that may vary.

Yet the truth of yesterday can be different from that of today.

It was and will always be true that I once lived in the mountains of Arizona. Yet the truth now is that I live in Southern California. The question now is, "By which truth do I actually live?"—the past truth or the current truth? If I live by the past truth, I'll find myself at the beach wearing a snowsuit, a large down-filled coat, and snowshoes. Not only will I look quite strange, I will *be* quite strange.

Principle: We must live according to current truth, or the past will distort our lives and rob us of what rightfully belongs to us.

This principle of truth applies to all areas of our lives.

Borrowing again from the Old Testament, we're admonished to walk in truth and be single-minded about it. "Teach me your way, O Lord, and I will walk in your truth; give me an undivided heart, that I may fear your name" (Ps 86:11).

Principle: The choice of a fully successful life is ours. So is the responsibility.

We're also told that walking according to the truth is a choice. "I have chosen the way of truth; I have set my heart on your laws" (Ps 119:30).

The Choice

This day I call heaven and earth as witnesses against you that I have set before you life and death, blessings and curses. Now choose life.
DEUTERONOMY 30:19-20a

Most of us have times when we become insecure, anxious, or angry. Yet to remain in these or other states of weakness is both unnecessary and wrong. When we do, it's typically because we don't recognize the weaknesses and haven't learned how to conquer them. This leaves us living at a level of mere survival.

Our weaknesses are robbing us of life and freedom and we don't even know it. What we should be doing is regathering our energies, draining them out of weaknesses, and redirecting them into developing strengths. When we do this, we can starve weaknesses to death and live abundantly. To invest in one is to destroy the other.

In the Old Testament passage above there are only two choices. One is life. The other is death. The choices aren't survival and death. They're life and death. Those of us who've struggled with weaknesses know much about survival and little about life. Yet we aren't supposed to settle for survival! We're intended to live life at its fullest.

Life is a banquet that we've been invited to attend. Weakness and survival would have us stop just outside the door. They'd convince us we're not worthy of the invitation. They'd have us feel too uncomfortable to attend. Once inside, they'd have us preoccupied with analyzing our discomfort. Weakness and survival would have us camouflage our real thoughts. They'd have us stand in the corner and contemplate those weaknesses. They'd have us pretend to be what we're not so that we'll be accepted.

Why does all of this happen? Somewhere along the way we've acquired weaknesses as survival techniques. Our weakness of continued denial saves us from looking at what we don't want to see and feeling what we don't want to feel. Our weakness of arrogance saves us from caring about rejection. Our weakness of perfectionistic attention to every detail makes us feel more secure. Our weakness of insecurity prompts us to please others so that we feel accepted. Our weakness of performance orientation gives us an identity in the absence of any real sense of self.

These thoughts and behaviors, originally intended for our protection, become our emotional prisons. They launch one self-fulfilling prophecy after another. Though they were once tools that we used to protect ourselves, they become weaknesses with which we destroy ourselves.

These weaknesses are not personality traits. They're not unalterable. For too long they've been hidden under the umbrella of temperament. Yet temperament is no excuse for weakness. Temperament is different from learned behavior. Learned thoughts and behaviors are the result of choice.

Remember that there are only two choices. We must choose one or the other. No one can remain neutral. To fail to choose life is to choose death, and survival is a type of seemingly acceptable death. It happens so slowly that we don't always see the inevitable results. We don't see our loss of joy or our forfeiture of success.

We're all affected not only by our own weaknesses but also by the weaknesses of others. So, it's important for us to be able to identify weaknesses both in ourselves and in others. To fail to identify weaknesses in ourselves and in others is to be doomed to live in reaction to those weaknesses and enslaved by them.

Have you chosen survival or life? Are you living a life subject to ongoing weaknesses, or are you living in freedom? Come along with me as we convert weaknesses from survival-level into strengths at the level of life!

ONE

Fear

I remember walking down a dark alley late at night. Halfway down the alley I saw, at a distance, a large dog chained to a metal post. I decided to walk on by as though I was unimpressed with him. I'm not sure what it was that gave me away, perhaps the deluge of sweat pouring from my brow. I was thinking, "I'm going to die. This is it! I'm some big dog's midnight snack! Just keep cool! Maybe he won't notice this trespassing biped in the middle of the night, in his own home territory."

Well, he saw me and I felt him see me. It gave me the shivers! The whole atmosphere changed. Nothing in the world existed but him and me. It was life or death. He was big and muscular enough to kill me. Without looking back at him, I heard him stealthily come to all fours. As I turned to run, he lurched into full attack.

Now, before I get too far into the story, I'd like to note a fine distinction between myself and the dog. I was a cross country runner. He was a sprinter. That's an important distinction at a time like this. Sprinters get there quickly. Cross country runners get there eventually. It seemed to me that, given that distinction, there was going to be a problem in the case of the dog and me. I wasted little time giving that distinction much consideration and set my mind upon learning the fine art of sprinting, post haste. Never could it have more aptly been said, "Use it or lose it!"

I'd always wondered if I'd be able to scream if I needed to. Well, yes I can. I found I could sprint, too. Lightning would have had to catch up with me on that night as I raced away from the dog. I heard the chain snap against the pole and the dog yelped. The chain had stopped him.

It felt like days before my adrenaline stopped pumping! Eventually, however, all of the fear subsided, and I determined, in the future, to avoid the combination of dark alleys and dogs on chains. I hold to that determination to this very day!

It's the nature of being human to be acquainted with fear. We fear the dark, mad dogs, nightmares, and bad hair days—the latter being the most frightening!

Yet there's a difference between an occasional justified fear, like the near miss on the highway, and the weakness of persistent or pervasive fear that extends beyond the point of reason. It's the latter at which we'll look in this chapter.

Deep Inside I'm Afraid
Weaknesses: Excessive or Unwarranted
Fears of Rejection or Abandonment

My grade school class decided to put on a play about American history. Students lined up against the blackboard, volunteering for the roles. Some volunteered to be native Indians. Not me; I didn't want stuff on my face. Some wanted to be pilgrims. Not me; the costumes were scratchy. Some chose to be Jefferson or Lincoln and some the food-stuffs of the first Thanksgiving. One boy actually begged to be the turkey. I've wondered about him ever since. He's probably some gazillionaire computer geek now who secretly owns Alaska and all the salmon therein.

I was afraid I wouldn't remember my lines, and that everyone who saw the play would think I was stupid and reject me. So, I pursued the role of the Statue of Liberty, who only stood there, arm in the air, holding perfectly still. I figured I could do that.

Well! I wasn't alone in my thespian pursuit. Three similar chicken tots shared my interest in the role. Standing there against the blackboard, hopes soaring, competition stirring deep in our souls, I noticed myself becoming a bit taller, straighter, my raised arm taking on attributes of torch-bearing. It was sheer unabashed desperation for the part.

I got it! I stood there, silent, holding a stupid cardboard torch in the air until my arm almost fell off! I was a hit, although I teetered in a slight circular motion. Draped in a wrapping that itched like crazy, I crossed my eyes, held my breath, and turned blue. No one knows the extraordinary pains actors endure for the sake of the craft!

What lengths we go to in order to avoid rejection! Fear of rejection and its cohort, fear of abandonment, are common. When excessive and unwarranted, they become weaknesses, barricades to success in life. Jill is a good example.

Jill

Today, Jill and her husband Kevin share a marriage of strength and trust that other couples envy. Yet there were once weaknesses standing in the way. They came to me with Kevin's concerns about Jill's jealousy and rage.

"She accuses me of not loving her, of wanting to leave her, of having affairs," Kevin broke down. "I tell her I love her, how wonderful she is, but nothing sticks. She doesn't believe me! I've never been unfaithful, not once!"

Jill didn't know why she was doing these things, but she knew she was afraid of losing Kevin, who'd given no indication of wanting to leave her. Her fears were driving her insatiable demand for absolute assurance he wouldn't leave. His reassurance could never resolve her fears. Her fears weren't new. She'd been clingy and jealous in previous relationships. Her fears existed before Kevin. It wasn't about him. It was about Jill.

What's the origin of these fears of rejection or abandonment?

Actual or perceived rejection or abandonment in the recent or distant past. When someone experiences a global, pervasive reaction like Jill's, often the source of that reaction is in the person's more distant past. This was true with Jill. When she was five years old her parents died in an airplane crash. Ever since the accident, Jill had feared that those she loved would leave her.

Many others, through divorce or death, have lost a parent or parent figure at an early age. The effects can be devastating. When we're children, our parents are our world, our security, and the most important people in our lives. If we lose either of them, our sense of security may be shattered.

Our ability to trust in the permanency of anyone in our lives may be damaged, since those who promised to take care of us are gone. We may feel rejected, because we're too young to understand loss. All we can see is that they've left us. These same reactions can occur to varying degrees with other types of rejection or abandonment.

When significant individuals don't emotionally invest in us, or they abuse us. Since we get our self-definition from our parents, their neglect or abuse may cause us to see ourselves as unworthy of attention or support, or worthy of being abandoned or abused. We may fear those circumstances reoccurring.

If someone leaves us when we're older, with no history of rejection or abandonment, the effects are different. Our fear of abandonment or rejection is narrower. We may avoid only those with similarities to the one who abandoned us, instead of distrusting people in general.

Some fears of rejection or abandonment are warranted. If someone has left us before, it makes sense that we may fear their leaving again. Most of that fear will go away if that person stays long enough. If someone constantly threatens to leave us, our fears will remain until the threats stop and the person stays for an extended period of time.

Other fears may be warranted but excessive. If one person rejects us, and we fear that all people will reject us, that fear is excessive. If one person abandons us, then returns and remains, yet we refuse to trust again, our fear is excessive.

How do we overcome the weaknesses of excessive or unwarranted fears of rejection or abandonment?

▶ *If possible, determine the source of the fear and when it began.* We need to find out where the fear came from, and when it started. Jill's fears originated with the loss of her parents in her childhood.

▶ *Determine if the fear makes sense in the current situation.* In her current situation, had Jill's husband given her any reason to fear he might abandon her? No. Based on that answer, her current fear of abandonment was unwarranted.

▶ *Take action.* If fear isn't warranted in the current situation, refuse to entertain it. The instant you become aware of the fear, redirect your thoughts to something else. This robs the fear of the mental or emotional fuel needed to maintain it.

Whenever Jill fears being rejected or abandoned, she stops and determines if the current situation alone warrants fear. If not, she knows it's her past fear making its way into a current situation. Jill then refuses to entertain these fearful thoughts, redirecting her thoughts elsewhere. By doing this, Jill relegates childhood fears of abandonment to the past, where they belong. At the same time she's building trust in her husband's commitment to her. Over time, the weakness has disappeared, replaced with trust based on truth. She now lives free of these fears and understands herself better. The fuel of her weakness now fuels her strength as she lives according to current truth instead of limited childhood perceptions. She lives by a principle: Never let fears live any longer than it takes to conform them to current truth.

Companion Weaknesses

1	6	11	16	21√	26√	31√	36√	41√	46√
2√	7√	12√	17√	22√	27√	32√	37	42	47√
3√	8√	13√	18	23√	28√	33√	38√	43	48
4√	9	14√	19√	24	29	34√	39√	44√	49√
5√	10	15	20	25√	30	35√	40	45√	50√

I Don't Let People Get Close to Me
Weakness: Excessive or Unwarranted Fear of Intimacy

Do you remember this kids' game? One reaches out, touches the other, and says, "I touch you." Then the one touched reverses the process, touching the other kid back, saying, "I touch you back." This continues until one final swat ends the play.

In this game, neither kid wants to have any real contact. The point of the game revolves around the invisible line they've drawn over which neither one is to venture without consent. This skirmish is reminiscent of what adults do when there's a problem with intimacy.

The fear of intimacy is a weakness with painful consequences. Ron's story is one example.

Ron

Ron wasn't the one who came to therapy, in the beginning. It was Megan, his wife, who came to the office with the look of confusion and pain common among those in love with someone who fears intimacy. She couldn't understand the arguments, the distancing, and the criticism, which were often preceded by wonderful closeness.

According to Megan, this was a pattern that had occurred throughout the three years of their marriage, and even before. Just before the wedding, Ron disappeared for several days, saying he just needed to get away and think. He called while away, assuring her of his love for her and sounding even more in love than when he left.

Early in the marriage Ron began to work late, coming home grumpy. Within two years he was drinking. Arguments escalated, with Ron often storming out and remaining away for days. While away, Ron missed Megan, calling her and coming home to deep, satisfying intimacy. Then the cycle would repeat: closeness, grumpiness, criticism of Megan, working late, alcohol, a big explosion, and Ron's leaving again.

Megan's heart was being torn apart. She loved Ron and knew he loved her. That was what was so hard to understand. Why would someone who couldn't think of living without her have to get away from her?

Ron was a good man and didn't understand why he treated Megan this way. He just knew that he felt smothered and had to get away. When he felt that way, everything about Megan bothered him, and he felt suffocated. After some time, Ron disclosed that this pattern had been a part of his relationships previous to Megan. Things were beginning to make sense.

Certainly Ron was capable of intimacy. Yet he could tolerate only so much intimacy before having to run away. This push-pull behavior, in which he was, in effect, saying, "Come close to me, but don't get near me!" was causing Megan great confusion and deep emotional pain.

Underneath Ron's fear of intimacy was a fear of commitment. When he got close to Megan he felt trapped. When he ran, it was not from her, but from commitment. While away he felt less trapped and could reach out to Megan again. He ran away by staying late at work, leaving town, or escaping into alcohol. His criticisms of her were intended to get her to distance herself from him, so he could breathe. Ron's fear of commitment drove his fear of intimacy, almost destroying his marriage.

What are the origins of the fear of intimacy?

Fear of loss of freedom, of change, or of commitment. Ron's fear of intimacy, undergirded by his fear of commitment, originated over a period of years. He came from a home where his mother did everything for him. He was catered to and given his full freedom. His mother still catered to him, and he didn't want things to change.

Lack of familiarity with intimacy. Some of us fear intimacy because it's unfamiliar. We didn't see it modeled in our families. It's a skills deficit. We haven't learned how to be intimate.

Fear of losing opportunities to be with others or of making a mistake. We may fear that there are others to whom we may be drawn yet will not be able to have. We may fear mistakenly choosing the wrong person.

Fear of losing ourselves. For some of us, underneath our fear of intimacy is a greater fear of losing ourselves. We're afraid to give ourselves away. We lack a solid sense of who we are, and we fear that if we give ourselves away, we'll lose who we are.

Fear of losing control, being exposed, or being hurt. For some of us intimacy sparks a fear of losing control. We may also have been hurt before and fear that intimacy will make us vulnerable once again to rejection, abandonment, or betrayal. We may fear that intimacy will expose us, or reveal that we're not good enough. We may not want to risk someone validating our negative self-appraisal.

In all of these scenarios, our fear of intimacy protects us from an anticipated harm. It protects us from emotional discomfort and leaves us in control. Yet it also stands in the way of true fulfillment in relationship. How to we overcome this weakness of fear of intimacy?

▸ *Recognize and admit our need for intimacy.* We need to recognize and admit to ourselves that we desire intimacy. If we didn't want it, we wouldn't let others get close enough for us to have to run away. Once we admit our fear of intimacy, we must challenge it. We need to determine why we're afraid, and what we're afraid of. Are these rational fears, or are we using our fear as an excuse to avoid responsible behavior?

▸ *Make lists.* We need to make a list of the problems that running from intimacy causes. Then we must anticipate how our lives will look if we continue to run from intimacy, and how they'll look if we choose a committed relationship.

▸ *Compare.* We must compare the pain of repeatedly losing relationships to the adjustment of accepting a lasting, loving relationship.

▸ *Recognize.* We need to recognize that our pain is self-inflicted, caused by our excessive concern with ourselves at the expense of investing in others. Once we've faced the truth that we're ensuring for ourselves shallow and alienated lives if we continue to subject ourselves to the fear of intimacy, then we can begin to change and to embrace the thought of how love and loving may change our lives and set us free.

▸ *Resist.* We must resist the urge to run when it arises. We must direct our thoughts to something else. The urge will cease if it is starved of attention.

▸ *Redirect.* Finally, we must redirect the energies once invested in running away into building relationships.

Though it wasn't easy, Ron conquered his fear of intimacy. In the long run his weakness of fearing intimacy was starved into submission as his energies were redirected to developing the strengths of concern for and interest in others. Ron finally came to understand that his intense focus on himself and his own concerns had become a prison that eventually only he would inhabit, unless he began to care more for others than he did for himself.

Companion Weaknesses

1N	6	11	16	21	26	31	36	41N	46√
2	7N	12	17	22	27	32N	37	42	47
3N	8	13	18	23	28	33	38	43N	48
4N	9	14N	19N	24	29	34	39N	44	49N
5	10	15	20	25	30N	35	40N	45	50N

I Can't Get Beyond the Memories of My Loss
Weakness: Excessive or Unwarranted Fear of Loss

I used to have a black box with a lock on it. Inside I kept all of my important keepsakes. Because it held important things, I became very protective of it. Just the thought of it could bring anxiety. Over time I removed the items in the box, as each item became less important to me. Eventually all that I had left was the box, yet it was the hardest thing of all to let go of. That's how our memories are, sometimes. They're all we have left of someone or something, and we find it hard to let go of them for that very reason. Let me use Beth as an example here.

Beth

Beth's contribution to grief counseling is enormous. She has helped many people recover from grief and loss and move on to healthy, productive lives. Many have looked to her to learn how to find strength to carry on in the face of loss. Yet, there was a time when weakness kept Beth from her own recovery.

"It's been three years now," Beth began. "We've been divorced for three years and I still think about him every day. I'm losing my friends because they're getting tired of hearing about Ed. The kids are getting tired of it, too."

Beth was holding on to her painful memories because they were all she had left of Ed. To let go of the memories would mean that she had to let go of Ed and move on. The loss was no longer the problem. It was the failure to let go. Her fear of loss was unwarranted because the loss had already occurred. What was left was only a memory, which she wasn't at risk of losing.

Beth, without realizing it, was using her memories of Ed to protect herself from becoming involved in another relationship and from the risk of losing again. She was choosing to live in self-produced and self-maintained pain as a way of avoiding the possibility of other types of pain. Had she not decided to change her thinking, her self-inflicted pain could have become permanent.

This same thing can happen to us when people hurt us or let us down. When we hold memories in our minds so we don't have to get over our pain and move on, it's our way, subconsciously, of punishing those who've hurt us, of still holding them accountable. Yet, most often these people don't even know we're doing this. They've moved on. We're the ones who are stuck, because we've decided to hold a grudge. Take a look at what Allen was doing before he turned his own fear of loss into the courage to move on.

Allen

Allen had been hurt by his boss at a company in which Allen owned part interest. He had been reprimanded in front of the whole management team, and his reputation had been seriously damaged. In his hurt and anger, Allen allowed his productivity to deteriorate.

"Why should I make him so much money?" Allen pouted. "After what he's done to me, why should I bring in big numbers just to let him destroy what's left of my dignity?"

Allen's income was based on those numbers, however, and to produce less in order to hurt his co-owner was to cut his own income, which he used to provide for his own family. Fear of future loss was leading Allen to self-sabotage. By punishing his boss he was punishing himself.

Allen couldn't get an apology from his boss, and he felt that keeping his production up was conceding that what his boss had said was right. He wasn't going to let that happen. Instead he slipped into depression and financial distress, all of his own doing. Holding on to his memory of the incident seemed to justify his anger, disappointment, and failure.

We hold on to our memories of loss because we think that somehow they'll protect us from further pain. Yet pain and life are inescapably connected. To master one we must master the other.

The excessive fear of loss becomes a weakness that keeps us mired in the losses its isolation brings, and causes us to merely survive, rather than live our lives to the fullest.

What are the origins of the weakness of excessive or unwarranted fear of loss?

Previous loss. We may have already suffered a loss, which sparks fear of future losses. This was the case with Beth.

Threats. We may be in a relationship with someone who threatens to leave. We may have a boss who threatens to fire us. We may be struggling with the impending loss of someone or something. This was Allen's story.

Valuing. We may anticipate loss when we have something or someone we cherish. The value of the thing or the person may drive the fear. The fear may prompt us to take precautions that simple reason would contend against.

How, then, do we combat excessive or unwarranted fear of loss?

▶ *Recognize and acknowledge.* We must recognize and acknowledge, first, that we're afraid. Then we must determine what it is that we're afraid of losing. This was an important step for Beth, who was unaware of why she was holding on to her memories of loss and pain.

▶ *Evaluate.* We need to determine if this fear is warranted, based on the current facts. Both Beth and Allen had to accept that loss was a part of life and that they could handle it. Beth had no reason to fear any imminent loss. Allen had to realize that his dignity was in his own hands, and that he could control his losses in that area. He therefore had no reason to fear.

▶ *Take action.* If the fear is warranted, we must take steps to deal with the potential loss. However, neither Beth nor Allen had fear that was warranted. If the fear isn't warranted, we must distract our thoughts from our fears and invest them in more productive pursuits.

Beth focused on moving on. She diverted the energy she was investing in fear of loss into recovering and developing the strength of compassion for others who have suffered loss. The fear of loss was deprived of the energy it needed to survive, and Beth moved gracefully from survival into the fullness of life.

Allen redirected the energies he'd invested in fear of loss into increasing his productivity and strengthening his character. In challenging his unwarranted fear of loss Allen learned that he relied too much on what others thought. He invested his rerouted energy into the strength of honest and accurate self-evaluation. He also began to develop the strength of humility as he learned to respect those in positions of authority over him.

Companion Weaknesses

1√	6	11	16	21√	26	31	36	41√	46
2√	7√	12	17	22	27	32√	37	42	47√
3	8	13	18	23	28	33√	38√	43√	48
4√	9	14	19	24	29	34√	39√	44√	49
5√	10	15√	20	25	30√	35	40√	45	50√

I'm Always Alert to Potential Dangers
Weakness: Excessive or Unwarranted Fears of Potential Harm

I have brothers. I can't help that. I was born that way. If you have older brothers, you're probably aware of their particular gifts and talents. One of those talents is the ability to jump out from behind any available hiding place and scream in your face. I'm not sure why boys do that. I think it's that hunting and gathering thing. They jump out from behind a tree and scare their prey to death. Regardless of why my brothers would do that, the result was always the same. I'd freeze in my tracks, scream loudly, and be sorely tempted to have a heart attack.

That little exercise wasn't performed often, but with enough frequency that for some time afterward, shrubs and trees without a clear view sparked my caution. Certainly I love my brothers and understand that boys will be boys. Yet this is an example of how repeated encounters with fearful circumstances may encourage us to be needlessly frightened. It can happen in any realm—emotionally, psychologically, physically, or even spiritually. With Jim, the catalyst was past fear of physical and emotional retaliation.

Jim

Jim has a calmness about him that's soothing to all those around him. He trusts others unless they give him reason not to, and he no longer lives in the land of secrets. Yet that's not the way things have always been. For many years Jim's weakness of unwarranted fear of potential harm kept him from the life that rightfully belonged to him.

In the beginning, talking to Jim was like trying to capture fog. He was so evasive with his responses that it was impossible to get a clear answer from him. If you watched closely you could almost see him editing every thought, changing this one, excluding that one.

Jim existed in a state of unnecessary guardedness. His internal agenda was self-protection through nondisclosure. He called it his need for privacy, but that's not what it was. He was struggling with an excessive and unwarranted fear of potential harm that he thought exposure might bring. Where do excessive or unwarranted fears of potential harm come from?

Previous harm or threats of harm. We may have experienced previous harm or threats of harm. Abused children fear further abuse, and Jim was an abused child. While his mother worked in the evenings, Jim's alcoholic stepfather would drink himself into drunken rages and become abusive toward Jim.

"He used to threaten me all the time. He'd tell me that if I told my mother about his hitting me he'd leave us and take his paycheck with him," Jim explained. "Mom didn't make enough on her own. I knew we needed his paycheck. And Mom didn't want to be without him. So, I didn't say anything."

Abused children learn, either by force or by instinct, to conceal the truth of inflicted abuses and the self-protective thoughts that come along with them. Because they conceal these thoughts, they don't subject them to external objectivity, which might make these fears go away. So, the fears remain, fueling the guardedness.

As they grow up, abused children continue the secretive behavior. They may be having trouble with their spouses, but they don't tell anyone. They may be uncomfortable, but they don't tell anyone. They edit their thoughts so nothing is revealed. They do this because it's what they have taught themselves to do. They turn inward. Their behavior in the real world is dominated by thoughts ruled by another day and time. They perceive threats where threats don't exist, and they grant grandiose importance to these perceptions.

When we base our current thoughts and behavior on yesterday's problems, we create turmoil in our relationships. We don't trust people who are worthy of trust, because we don't need to. We've learned by concealing our thoughts that we don't need to trust.

Unfortunately, however, relationship is built on trust. Lack of trust leaves us in our own secret worlds and in relationships where we aren't emotionally there. Emotional presence requires spontaneity, and our internal editing and guardedness leave us several degrees removed from others. Others sense the distance but don't understand it. All they're left with is confusion and eventual anger.

How can we conquer this weakness of excessive or unwarranted fear of potential harm?

▶ *Recognize.* First, we need to recognize our fears of potential harm. We need to listen to others who are complaining of our guardedness and emotional distance, and recognize that our excessive or unwarranted fears of potential harm are actually harming others. If we don't want to become the ones who now cause the harm, we must eliminate our excessive fear and the guardedness it creates.

▶ *Externalize.* It's important for us to externalize our internal fears and subject them to outside evaluation. Jim learned to say out loud what he feared. He could then get feedback from objective individuals whose continued and consistent responses showed him that he had no real reason to be afraid. This opening up to others allowed Jim to begin to develop the strength of trust.

▶ *Redirect.* If our fears aren't based in reality, we need to reinvest our thoughts and emotional energies elsewhere. Over time Jim became comfortable with those against whom he had previously guarded himself. The emotional energy he'd once used to protect himself was redirected into developing those relationships.

▶ *Resolve.* If our fears are valid, we must take steps to deal with the real potential of being harmed. Jim found that when he subjected his fears of potential harm to objective review, his unwarranted fears of harm evaporated. That left previously committed emotional and intellectual energies free to invest in developing the strengths of trust and responsible risk-taking.

Companion Weaknesses

1√	6√	11√	16	21√	26	31√	36	41	46
2√	7√	12√	17	22√	27	32√	37	42	47√
3√	8√	13√	18	23√	28	33	38√	43√	48
4	9	14√	19√	24	29	34	39√	44√	49√
5√	10	15√	20	25	30√	35	40√	45	50√

I'm Afraid to Try

Weakness: Excessive or Unwarranted Fears of Failure or Success

Few things strike terror in my heart more swiftly than long division. I think this fear arose when as a child my family moved and I entered a new school where long division had already been taught. I'd awaken in the night with fears of having to go to the blackboard and divide one number by another. I was so frightened by the possibility of the experience that I froze, unable for a long time to learn long division.

Prior to that point, I'd been able to learn all I'd been taught, so there was no need for my fear. Yet as a child I didn't understand that it was going to take time to acquire this skill. I thought I had to learn it immediately. I was afraid of failing.

Still, I had no choice but to make the attempt. Had I not jumped in and taken the risk, my fear of failure might have actually produced failure. That's one of the attributes of fear. Left unchallenged, it tends to be self-fulfilling. Our fears of failure or success can be debilitating. Ed is a perfect example.

Ed

Ed is currently at the top of his region and second in the nation in sales for his company. Yet, this wasn't always the case.

At my first meeting with Ed and his wife, Joyce, she told me, "He's busy doing nothing. He's taking care of the backyard and fixing up the garage. Bills are going unpaid and he gets mad if I suggest his getting a job. I think he's just afraid of failing."

Where do fears of failure or success originate?

Lack of familiarity with success or failure, or experience in either area. Perhaps we're unfamiliar with failure or success, or we've had previous disappointments in one of those areas. Ed was the top salesman in the region until his new boss reduced his territory. Ed's income plummeted. In his despondency he started missing work.

Ed began to struggle with fears of both failure and success. He was afraid that he might not be able to reach the heights he'd once attained, that perhaps he no longer had the strength to get there. Yet, he also feared that he might succeed, and that success would bring with it all of the responsibilities he'd recently relinquished.

Now these competing fears were leading him to procrastinate. Furthermore, Ed was struggling with resentment about having been treated unfairly. Together, these factors combined to produce paralysis, causing Ed to lose much of what he'd worked for.

Perfectionism. Perfectionism may also be a culprit. Ed's original success had been fueled by perfectionism and his need to earn the approval of all those around him. Deprived of attention and the approval of his father when he was growing up, Ed had sought to earn approval by doing things well. Because his father was not responsive to his efforts, Ed had continually felt the need to do even more in the attempt to earn approval, eventually becoming a perfectionist.

Because perfectionism was the force behind Ed's previous success, he'd never really accepted his success. Perfectionism works on the fear that what is done is never good enough. That's what propels the perfectionist to greater heights. Ed had made it to the top without developing genuine confidence in himself.

Now Ed was languishing in fear, mistakenly thinking that he would have to start all over again. Yet he was failing to see that he had plenty of experience under his belt that would make this current road to success much less intimidating. Furthermore, because he had been successful before, he had nothing to prove this time. The question this time was the quality of his success, not the quantity. This time his success, rather than being based on unmet needs for approval and attention, would be based on truth and real confidence. This time, success would not be the goal. It would be the byproduct. He knew that the product he was selling was excellent. He believed that the product was good for people. He began to sell the product for them, not for himself.

Principle: To do what is right for others is to do what is right for ourselves.

He forgave the boss who had reduced his territory. He could then move on without being fused to the pain of past experiences.

How can we turn the weaknesses of fear into strengths?

▶ *Follow God's example.* The smartest thing to do is to follow the best example. On a number of occasions God told us how to feel! He said, "Do not be afraid!" Perhaps the earliest example of this is found in Genesis: "*After this, the word of the Lord came to Abram in a vision: 'Do not be afraid, Abram. I am your shield, your very great reward'*" (Gn 15:1).

Other examples may be found throughout the Old Testament (see, for example, Gn 21:17, 46:3; Ex 14:13; Dt 3:22; Jos 10:8; 2 Chr 32:7; and Is 43:5).

Notice that when God told people not to be afraid, he followed it up with the reason why they had no need for fear. God's solution for fear was trust in him. In this way, he told us how to handle our fears. He moved us ahead of our fears to our future. Our trust was to be in his promise for a planned outcome.

▶ *Plan.* Fears flourish due to a lack of planning. We need to answer the question "What if ...?" We need to view our fears as possible eventualities and plan for how we'll deal with them, should they occur. In doing so, we'll be looking past our fears to their solutions. Once we're prepared for any eventuality, the need for fear will disappear, replaced by confidence in having planned a solution. Here's the formula:

Take feared circumstances ——▶ *See them as possible eventualities* ——▶ *Determine plans of action* ——▶ *The reasons for the fears will disappear* ——▶*Replaced with confidence in our ability to handle the future!*

▶ *Face the truth.* We must be honest, with ourselves and with others. Ed faced the fact that he knew how to become successful and had done it before. He realized that he was going to have to spend his time doing something. In light of this fact, doing something productive was more personally rewarding than sitting around feeling guilty. The prospect of dealing with the challenges of success began to appeal to him once more. He knew that he could summon up the energy to push for success because he remembered that in the past the challenges had actually energized him. He no longer needed to fear success. He didn't need to be afraid, because he knew what he was doing.

The same formula works for those who haven't experienced a major success or failure and fear either one. The way to eliminate these weaknesses is to anticipate that what we're afraid of may happen, then devise a plan for how to handle it if it does. Once we're prepared for these eventualities, the fear surrounding them will evaporate.

As we accept our fears and plan our actions in the face of these fears, we'll develop the strength of confidence in ourselves to handle the future. With this strength will come the strength of courage to take risks.

Companion Weaknesses

1√	6√	11√	16	21√	26√	31	36√	41√	46
2√	7√	12√	17√	22√	27√	32√	37	42	47√
3√	8√	13√	18√	23√	28√	33√	38√	43√	48
4√	9	14√	19√	24	29	34√	39√	44	49√
5	10	15√	20√	25√	30	35√	40√	45√	50√

TWO

Anxiety

If you were the kind of child I was, we both should be paying for our mothers' anxiety and high blood pressure medications. It's one thing for me to see my life through my own eyes, and quite another to see it through my mother's eyes. I don't mean perspective either. I'm literally talking about what my mother saw. Let's go behind my mother's eyeballs for a moment and look out at what we'd see.

There we'd be, looking out the window on a beautiful summer day, when suddenly out of nowhere something outside would pass so swiftly that we'd question what it was. Was that our precious little daughter riding at the speed of a violent wind past the window on a horse, bareback no less? Why yes, we believe it would be. Anxiety attack number seven thousand three hundred sixty-four! And were those her red Keds sneakers we saw wobbling past the window on those six-foot stilts? Why yes, we believe they would be. Anxiety attack number seven thousand three hundred sixty-five! Was that our daughter sitting up in that tall tree? Clinging like a cat, halfway up the chain-link fence? Inner-tubing down the river? Hiking off on a trail all by herself? I think that gives you the general idea.

So, how was it, back there behind Mother's eyeballs? It was a little bit nerve-wracking, wasn't it? I know it was for her. Thank God for her faith! (Now that I think of it, I should be given a good deal of credit for the growth of my mother's faith.)

There are times when anxiety is a natural response to a triggering situation. We drop a vase, try to catch it, and for a split second we feel the sharp pang of anxiety. It's there when we take a driving test, when we go on a first date, when we go to the dentist, or when relatives call to say they're visiting.

Anxiety was intended to be an indicator, not a tool. It's intended to alert us to something that needs attention. When we allow anxiety to outlive that purpose, it eventually becomes an unhealthy motivational tool. When that happens, we need to determine if the thing that our anxiety motivates us to do is right and reasonable. If it is, we need to use some other means to motivate ourselves to do it, not anxiety.

When anxiety becomes a tool, it becomes a part of our lifestyle. Anxiety is intended to be short-lived and occasional, not constant. Yet, for some of us, anxiety lives just beneath the surface, gnawing at our souls and never completely leaving us alone. We've formed an alliance with it, and contracted it to be a motivational force in our lives.

When I Slow Down I Feel Anxious
Weakness: Performance Orientation

There are many things for which I'm thankful. Among them are God's grace, his mercy, good friends, and negative people. Whenever I'm ready for more growth, some negative person will step up to the plate and help me see my next area of needed improvement.

One of the wonderful things about negative people is that you never have to call room service and order one up. They just always seem to be around. Isn't that just swell? Yet, while we might have the urge to avoid the negative people in our lives as often as we can, it would be a mistake to ignore them completely. Over the years I've discovered that negative people are like bad pennies—they show up in the oddest places, and often bring with them the beginnings of great wealth.

That's the way it was for me after an awards ceremony at a school I was attending. I'd just been awarded the school's highest honors, and was feeling very honored at receiving the award. The next day, I encountered a professor of mine in the hallway at school, and he commented on the award. I read positive things into his comments and responded.

"Thanks," I said. "Just wait until you see what I can do next year!"

With that, he threw his hands to the sky as if to ward off a demon, and said "WOOOOH!" It wasn't the kind of expression that says "How wonderful!" It was more like a Martian space saucer had just skidded up to his feet and the dust was flying everywhere. Then he quietly walked on. With that it finally dawned on me that he had the impression I was being a bit overzealous.

Over the years, I've found that I've not been the only person on planet earth who has had to contend with the weakness of performance orientation. Sally faced a similar struggle.

Sally

Sally is an extremely intelligent, highly verbal person. She's the president of her own company, she has a graduate degree in business management, and she skydives. Her sense of humor is incredibly sharp, with flawless timing. Come to think of it, Sally does everything almost flawlessly. So why wasn't she satisfied with her success, and why did she come to me so depressed?

For one thing, Sally was performance-oriented, and one of the costs of performance orientation is a lack of lasting satisfaction with success.

Many of us wonder why we don't enjoy the successes we achieve. Most often it's because we're driven to success by a performance orientation rather than by a simple pursuit of character development, of which success is a natural by-product.

To be driven to success by a performance orientation makes us vulnerable to disappointment upon obtaining that success. This happens because success is usually hollow if unaccompanied by maturity of character. If we're consumed by our drive to perform, we can't concentrate on character development. One occurs at the expense of the other. If our aim is success, that's all we'll get. If our aim is character, we'll get it all!

Performance won't provide lasting satisfaction. It's what we do, not who we are. It was Sally's performance orientation that was causing her problems and robbing her of satisfaction in life.

Where does the weakness of performance orientation originate?

Fear. There may be fear of repercussions. Sally developed a performance orientation early in life. Her father was controlling and perfectionistic. He criticized her relentlessly. Sally responded by trying harder to please him. The attempts were futile and repeated often enough for Sally to become performance-oriented.

Avoidance. Performance orientation may be a result of an attempt to avoid negative circumstances in our lives. In the beginning, Sally was performing, trying hard to please, in order to avoid her father's anger. She performed in order to protect herself.

A desire for security and well-being. Doing things well did keep Sally's father from becoming angry with her. For this reason, the constant striving to do well made her feel secure and safe, so she kept on doing it. She then began to equate her performance with well-being. As long as she was performing well she was OK.

Anxiety avoidance. The act of keeping busy calmed Sally's anxieties, even though it didn't resolve them. When she slowed down, she'd feel anxious. Eventually Sally found that she had to keep busy just to avoid the feelings of anxiety. Her performance orientation now served another purpose, calming her anxieties.

Approval-seeking. The better we perform, the more praise we receive. Once again, the performance orientation serves multiple purposes.

Identity. Repeated praise and reward for performance encourages more performance. If the praise is absent in other areas of our lives, we may over-identify with performance and see that as our source of identity.

Since performance doesn't bring resolution, anxiety and fear beneath the performance orientation continue to build. One thing is compounded upon another and the weakness of performance orientation grows.

Sally had become performance-oriented and anxiety driven. Those weaknesses lived on long after she'd moved away from her family. Neither of these tendencies was easy to overcome, but with patience and determination, she did it.

Remember that performance orientation occurs under the pressure of anxiety or fear. They become our motivators. In overcoming performance orientation, we must limit fear and anxiety to their intended roles. We do this by not allowing fear and anxiety to propel us into action. To do this, we must:

▶ *Stop at the point of the urge.* When we feel the urge to do something, we need to stop for a few moments and do nothing. The anxiety or fear will roll over us like a wave, and then we'll feel a sense of relief for a few seconds. Those few seconds of relief are what real life is supposed to feel like.

▶ *Identify.* We need to try to identify the motivator. The feeling that will roll over us will likely be either anxiety or fear. Anxiety is a feeling of being ill at ease or emotionally uneasy. Fear is a heavier feeling that carries with it a sense of desperation or dread.

▶ *Track it down.* Determine the origin of the fear or anxiety. Did it start with the current situation or some time before?

▶ *Challenge.* Challenge the anxiety or fear. Does this anxiety or fear make sense in this specific situation?

▶ *Act.* Act on a decision instead of an urge. Once we've paused and the anxiety has gone its way, we need to think about what it was that we were about to do. If we still want to do it, then we need to decide to do it and act on our decision, thus eliminating the survival behavior of performance orientation as we learn to discipline ourselves to make responsible decisions.

This is exactly what Sally did. Eventually she began to experience a sense of calm in her life. She made decisions about doing things instead of doing things as a result of being driven by fear or anxiety. When her emotional and mental energy was drawn away from the weakness of performance orientation and focused into facing her fears and anxieties, Sally's life became satisfying. She began to develop the strengths of character and responsible decision making.

Companion Weaknesses

1√	6	11√	16	21√	26√	31√	36	41	46
2√	7√	12√	17	22√	27√	32√	37	42	47√
3√	8√	13√	18√	23√	28	33√	38√	43	48
4√	9	14√	19	24	29	34√	39√	44	49√
5√	10	15	20	25	30	35√	40	45√	50√

Give Me Peace at Any Cost
Weakness: Pervasive Conflict Avoidance

Many times as a child I was concerned about my father becoming angry. I became quite sensitive to his moods and was able, even as a child, to tell when he was on edge. At those times, I'd be quiet, invisible if possible. When I could I'd arrange to be somewhere else. Yet there were times when I wasn't able to be elsewhere and had to remain in the tension-filled environment. Some of the most difficult times were those when my father was in a bad mood and my mother was having difficulty with him.

I'd see that my mother was on the verge of saying something that would set him off. I'd do anything I could to try to distract her, to keep her from saying something that would ignite the spark for which we'd all pay. In the back of my mind I'd be saying "No, Mom! Don't say anything! Please, just don't say anything!"

I'd try to keep the conflict from escalating. I couldn't get away. I couldn't control my dad. So, I'd try to protect my mother from herself and to protect myself from any further emotional trauma. All of this I knew I was doing, yet I didn't realize how very controlling I was becoming.

I was trying, indirectly, to control my circumstances and the people in them from behind the scenes. I would pretend to be interested in something in order to draw my mother's attention to it and away from the tension. I was concerned about her and about Dad, but most of all I didn't want to go through any more trauma. I was trying to control them in order to ease my own fears.

I wouldn't suggest that what I did was wrong. As a matter of fact, I think it was wise, in those circumstances. Yet, as is generally true with survival behaviors, when those years of conflict were over, the tendency to control in order to avoid conflict was still there. Now I had weaknesses on my hands, controlling and conflict avoidance.

I've found, over the years I've been a therapist, that most conflict-avoidant individuals are unaware of their own motives and their own maneuvering to control others. I think this happens because we define conflict as bad and use that definition as our justification to do whatever we think necessary to avoid it. Yet, avoiding conflict can also have negative repercussions. Take a look at what happened to Kevin.

Kevin

Kevin is a salesman who for about four years had seen a serious decrease in his income. He, his wife Angela, and their two adopted children were living in a beautiful dream home they'd purchased just before Kevin's sales dwindled. To the outside world this looked like the ideal family. Yet that wasn't the case.

For some time Kevin had been draining the family's savings to offset business losses. All the while, the family had been going on expensive vacations, lavishing gifts at Christmastime, and keeping up appearances. Kevin didn't want to face the disappointment in his wife's eyes, or see his children leave private colleges. So, he kept what he was doing to himself.

Angela sensed that something was wrong but couldn't figure it out.

She asked about finances, and Kevin's response was always that things were fine. At some point Angela decided she didn't want to know what the problem was. She didn't want anything to change her ideal world. Then came the call that changed it all.

Early one morning a collection agency called, asking for Kevin. Angela took the call. They were after a sizable sum that Kevin was late in paying.

"Are you sure you have the right person?" Angela asked. "This can't be right." Yet it was.

When Kevin got home, Angela asked him about the call. He suggested they'd had the wrong number or that it had been for some other person by the same name. He continued this charade until other calls came in and his lies were no longer convincing. Angela went into quiet shock, waiting for the rest of the information.

Their liquid assets were gone. They were mortgaged to the maximum, and Kevin had no place to run. He threatened suicide and was hospitalized until stabilized. Two months later, under the stress, Angela suffered a heart attack and was hospitalized, though she did eventually recover.

Had it not been for Angela's wealthy father, Kevin and Angela would have lost everything, including their marriage. Angela's father bailed them out, saving their house, and even paying their medical bills. He arranged for Kevin to pay back what he could, and made therapy a condition of the arrangement. That brought them into my office.

There were many serious issues underlying this situation. All of them could've been dealt with, had Kevin and Angela not avoided conflict. All that was learned in therapy could've been learned without the crisis or the cost. Yet there was an error in their reasoning. Conflict had mistakenly been seen only as a detriment and not as a pathway to progress.

In avoiding conflict, Kevin's character took one hit after another. So did his family. He lied to them and broke their trust. He gave them false hope, and in his determination to avoid facing the conflict of financial constraints and an altered image, Kevin destroyed his family's seemingly ideal world.

What are the origins of conflict avoidance?

Fear. There may be a fear of repercussions. For Kevin, certainly his pride played a part in image becoming more important than substance. Yet, the primary motivation for his avoidance of conflict was fear. He feared the rejection of the community, the disappointment of his wife, and the rejection of his children.

Modeling. Conflict-avoidant behavior may also arise from the modeling of a significant person in our lives. Conflict avoidance is learned and can be changed.

How do we overcome the weakness of conflict avoidance?

▶ *Identify.* We must identify the motives behind our conflict-avoidant behaviors. They may seem pure, yet that's often because those of us who are conflict-avoidant think we can't deal with conflict, so we justify what we do to make it acceptable. We may say that we're trying to keep the peace, yet our underlying motive may be to avoid the uncomfortable feelings that come with conflict and not being in control.

▶ *Understand.* We need to understand that conflict avoidance is not a personality trait. It's a tool we've developed in order to deal with things in our lives that cause us discomfort.

▶ *Truth.* In every situation we must tell the whole truth and challenge the value of conflict avoidance as a method or tool. A useful exercise would be to list the positive and negative results of using conflict avoidance as a method of dealing with issues, and assess its value. In Kevin's case the negative results of conflict avoidance were that conflict was never permanently avoided, only postponed. Furthermore, with postponement, the conflict escalated. Character was compromised in order to temporarily avoid discomfort. Significant long-lasting losses impacting the entire family were the result. There was no positive value in Kevin's conflict-avoidant behavior. Even if it diminished his initial anxiety, this was for only a brief period, followed by even greater anxiety. An honest assessment of Kevin's use of conflict avoidance shows it to be an unfortunate and costly choice.

▶ *Choose another method.* We must find other ways to resolve the underlying issues. If we can divert our energies from the weakness of conflict-avoidant behavior and reroute them into methods of productively resolving our conflicts, we'll find that our path through life is a much easier one.

It took a long time for Kevin to recover from his struggle with conflict avoidance. In the process, however, he learned to be honest about his motives and in his dealings. He grew to know himself better and began to make responsible choices. He faced his fears and developed the strengths of humility and courage. In so doing, he kept his family together.

Companion Weaknesses

1√	6√	11	16	21√	26√	31√	36	41√	46√
2√	7	12√	17	22√	27√	32√	37	42	47√
3√	8√	13√	18√	23√	28√	33√	38√	43√	48√
4√	9	14√	19	24	29	34√	39√	44	49√
5√	10√	15√	20√	25	30	35√	40	45√	50√

When I Do Well, I Think I Could Have Done Better
Weakness: Perfectionism

I had a fellow tell me once that he was perfect. It was a very short conversation. I didn't want to stand there and discuss the possible alternatives, so I just grinned and moved on.

I doubt this fellow was a perfectionist, because they're more subtle than that. They know and will even say they aren't perfect. Yet they often fool themselves with their near-perfect accomplishments. Here are the stories of two perfectionists. Both Stan and Marty struggled with perfectionism, but their struggles were quite different.

Stan

Stan loves it now when he comes home from work and his children jump all over him. Yet until he dealt with his weakness of perfectionism, his response was anger. Here's a look back.

"He never keeps his promises," Lanie said, "and his anger is getting out of control."

The look on Stan's face was stern determination, but behind that was the look of gnawing anxiety. It was the recognizable façade cloaking the unmet expectation of perfection. Self-defense wasn't far behind. Lanie, his wife, was used to it.

"That's an inaccurate statement," Stan said. "I do lots of things around the house."

"I'm not saying you don't do things around the house," Lanie responded. "You just don't finish things. Then you get mad at me if I bring it up and ask you to get it done."

"Maybe you don't realize all I do during the course of the day!" Stan said defensively. "I don't like your misrepresenting me this way. I get tired of all of the criticism."

Stan was demonstrating one of the characteristics of perfectionism, excessively high expectations leading to procrastination. Why do something if you can't do it perfectly, the thinking goes. What he saw as criticism was a plea from his wife for him to finish what he'd begun. But anything that called attention to imperfection on his part was an unbearable criticism, prompting anger and self-defense.

While Stan dealt with his perfectionism from a self-defensive posture, Marty was on the other side of the perfectionistic coin. His was the offensive, overtly aggressive response.

Marty

Marty often berated his wife: "Why can't you just clean up the house? Is that so hard? It's not like you have to be a rocket scientist! What's your problem?"

"He yells and says mean things to our son and to me," Jan related. "I hate that. He criticizes everything. He's sarcastic! If we interrupt what he's doing, he gets furious."

All of the perfectionistic demands, the absence of encouragement, and the complaints and criticisms left Peter, their seventeen-year-old son, bitter toward his dad. They also left him without respect for his mother. Unfortunately, Peter was carrying on the tradition by placing perfectionistic demands on his girlfriend and himself.

Jan and Peter both struggled with depression, not uncommon in a family under the tyrannical rule of perfectionism. The perfectionists themselves are as much under the rule of perfectionism as are the rest of the family. It's just that they have the power to put a stop to it, yet often don't know why they should.

What's the source of the weakness of perfectionism?

Excessively high expectations. Stan was raised by a perfectionistic father. Like his mother, he felt he didn't measure up, and his self-esteem collapsed. Eventually he became paralyzed when asked to do something. Having been hurt by so much of it, Stan also became excessively sensitive to criticism.

Modeled behavior. Marty also had perfectionistic parents. This was the only model of behavior presented to him. So far as he knew, perfectionistic expectations were normal, and he saw his wife and children as lazy and rebellious for not complying.

Attempts to earn approval and ward off rejection. If, in our childhood, we didn't get our approval needs met, we may try to earn that approval. If the need remains unmet we keep on trying and eventually develop a tendency toward perfectionism. This perfectionism continues into future relationships as we continue to try to earn approval.

So, how can we overcome the weakness of perfectionism?

▶ *Challenge.* We must challenge the notion of perfectionism and call it what it is. The premise of perfectionism—that things can be perfect—is false. No one is perfect. If the response is that we should still try, then we must look to the damage that perfectionism causes and ask ourselves if the notion of perfectionism is a good thing. It's not. It's a tyrant, because it demands the impossible. It shouldn't be a part of our lives, much less a goal. So, what's a reasonable goal in life? Maturity is a good choice, a range of thought and behavior that isn't perfect but, far more often than not, results in what's right and good for everyone.

▶ *Track it down.* We need to try to determine where the mistaken notion of perfection came from, and why it's there. Was perfectionism modeled to us when we were young? Were there repercussions if excessively high standards weren't met? Did we succumb to the notion in order to protect ourselves? Do we still need that protection today?

▶ *Learn to live with continuums.* Perfectionists view life in terms of rights and wrongs, black and white. It's important for us to develop a life with a middle ground, thinking along a continuum. A continuum is a sequence of change from one point to another.

If we were to make an anger continuum it would show the progression from feeling nothing to feeling rage. A non-perfectionist's continuum might read like this:

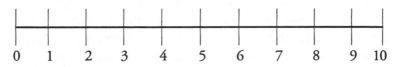

with the range of feelings, in order of escalation, as 0 = no feeling, 1 = a little bothered, 2 = annoyed, 3 = frustrated, 4 = irritated, 5 = angry, 6 = put out, 7 = smoldering, 8 = really upset, 9 = boiling, and 10 = rage.

The non-perfectionist experiences many of the nuances of feeling along the anger continuum. Certain circumstances may warrant irritation. Some may warrant being a little bothered, and some may warrant being very upset. Perfectionists, however, don't relate to the options.

Perfectionists tend to go from no feeling (0) to rage (10) very quickly, without relating to the nuances of feeling in between. The perfectionist's continuum is more like this:

Why is that? Why do perfectionists tend to escalate from 0 to 10 so quickly? The answer is that they're responding to their expectations of perfection, which are black and white, all or nothing at all. Something is either perfect or it's not. There are no shades of gray in perfection. Furthermore, perfectionists' continuums of expectations tend to be similar to those of their anger, moving rapidly from 0 (no expectation) to 10 (expectation of perfection). There's no middle ground.

In contrast, the continuum of expectations for non-perfectionists will look a little more like the first continuum above with the nuances of feeling, in order of escalation: 0 = no expectation, 1 = expectation of doing poorly, 2 = expectation of doing a bit better, 3 = expectation of greater progress, 4 = expectation of approaching average performance, 5 = expectation of average performance, 6 = expectation of above-average performance, 7 = expectation of doing very well, 8 = expectation of exceptional performance, 9 = expectation of outstanding performance, and 10 = expectation of excellence.

The continuums of the perfectionist allow no flexibility, no room for error. Those of us who struggle with the weakness of perfectionism therefore need to sit down and map out continuums in all areas of expectation, and to practice them. When we do, like turning the volume up and down, our emotions will begin to modulate with those expectations.

▶ *Do it now.* Procrastination, a hallmark of perfectionism, occurs for several reasons. Since our mandate is that things be done perfectly, we're reluctant to start projects. Furthermore, once we start them, the anxiety of the expectation of perfection pulls us back from the project. Once we have pulled back, the anxiety about finishing the project builds, and the project remains undone. If we finish the project at the last minute or late, we've learned to produce under pressure. We then wait until the last minute in every situation, in order to use that pressure as motivation. We're training ourselves to live at a high level of anxiety.

Instead of putting things off, we need to do just the opposite, make decisions and act on them as immediately as possible. Procrastination will give way to accomplishment.

Stan and Marty both had difficult tasks in front of them as they faced the weakness of perfectionism. What they'd thought was idealism or the norm beckoning them to perfection was in reality anxiety and fear trying to compensate for insecurity or to replicate a mistaken notion of what was normal.

Stan learned that it wasn't perfectionism that was keeping him from success. He was standing in his own way. He then accomplished the difficult task of accepting that he was his own harsh taskmaster, with the power to change his own behavior. He began to practice flexible expectations, eventually becoming comfortable with them. He redirected his vast emotional energy away from perfectionism and invested it instead in developing the strengths of reasonable self-discipline and in developing healthy relationships.

Marty learned that perfectionism destroys individuals and relationships with its unrelenting criticism. Deluded by his perfectionistic ability to achieve, Marty had slipped into a false sense of superiority, looking down upon others, and becoming impatient, controlling, and arrogant. He came to see those changes as indications of the failure of perfectionism. He then rerouted his emotional energies from perfectionism into the strengths of self-understanding and mercy.

Companion Weaknesses

1√	6√	11√	16	21√	26√	31	36√	41√	46√
2√	7√	12√	17√	22√	27√	32√	37√	42√	47√
3√	8	13√	18√	23√	28√	33√	38√	43√	48√
4√	9√	14√	19√	24√	29	34√	39√	44	49√
5√	10	15√	20√	25√	30√	35√	40√	45√	50√

If Things Get Calm I Start an Argument
Weakness: Crisis Orientation

When I was a child, my father would have the family run through fire drills. To this very day I have a plan of escape. In my current residence, I plan to hurl myself up against the double-paned window, either breaking through and plummeting to the shrubbery below or promptly bouncing back, semiconscious, onto the floor. Fortunately, however, I no longer practice fire drills, as practicing my current plan of escape would cut down drastically on my time at the office and would raise my medical bills significantly. (In reality I do have a plan of escape, should fire break out, and I think we should all have one.)

My mother was subject to the same fire drills as the rest of the family. For some reason, apparently, the drills didn't stick. Late one cold winter night, I was awakened by movement in the living room. In the shadowy light my mother was quietly throwing water from what looked like a drinking glass into the inside wall by the fireplace. This seemed odd to me as we didn't typically water our house. There was a glow coming from within the wall, and it looked to me that it might be on fire. Having been through numerous fire drills, I thought,

"Hmmmm. My mother is throwing a glass full of water onto the burning walls of the house. My father is asleep in one room and the kids in another. This doesn't seem to fit the fire drill plan."

My brother soon got up to lend a hand, by hauling water in a cooking pot. I thought this was brilliant, myself. Everybody should have a brother so smart! As the walls took on a larger, warmer glow, however, I began to wonder what Plan B might be.

I must admit, before I get you laughing too hard, and give you the impression that my mother was inept, that there were reasons why my mother was taking the minimalist approach to putting out the fire. My father was in an adjoining room, recovering from serious surgery, and my mother wanted desperately not to disturb him. She did, however, eventually call the fire department, and they arrived swiftly, though with sirens off so that they, too, would not cause my father any further pain.

Notice, however, throughout this episode, how calm I was. This is a common trait among those of us who've had turbulent or unpredictable backgrounds. We get used to crisis and learn to handle it well. While others go into hysteria, we go into cruise control.

We're good at crisis. We know what to do and how to make it through. Yet, some of us have experienced so much crisis that that's all we know how to do well. For this reason, we tend to create crisis. It helps us feel involved. It makes us feel alive, competent, capable, and important. Ellen is an excellent example of this.

Ellen

Ellen enjoys a loving relationship with her husband, Paul. They work together in their own business, moving it forward, enjoying the camaraderie. But it hasn't always been this way. There was a time when Ellen's weakness of crisis orientation was destroying her marriage.

In our first meeting Ellen and Paul sat on opposite ends of the couch, as if one or the other of them had rabies. Every time Paul would say something, Ellen would launch into an attack. She wasn't really being defensive because she wasn't trying to defend herself. She was just arguing because she could.

Why would someone create a crisis like that just because he or she could? In this case it was because Ellen had developed a crisis orientation in a previous relationship that had been abusive. With this weakness, which seemed to be invisible to her, Ellen was at risk of destroying her marriage.

During the course of therapy, Ellen had to learn how she had developed this weakness. Only then could she apply what she'd learned to transform her weaknesses into strengths.

Where does the weakness of crisis orientation originate?

A chaotic environment or relationship. We all have crises in our lives from time to time. That's normal. Yet some of us were raised in homes where there was a great deal of ongoing turmoil. Perhaps we were raised in an alcoholic home or one where a parent was perfectionistic or prone to rage. Perhaps we faced the loss of a parent, or lived in a home where there was chronic illness or an abusive sibling or parent. Others of us may have had a perfectly wonderful childhood, only to find ourselves in a chaotic or crisis-ridden relationship later on in life. Wherever or whenever we encounter repeated crisis, we're affected by it.

There are a number of dangers that arise when there's chronic crisis in our lives.

1.) Increased tolerance. With repeated or chronic crisis in our lives, our ability to tolerate crises increases. We become more comfortable with them and begin to experience them as normal. For this reason, we tend to be drawn to crisis or to cause crises, in order to create an environment that feels normal to us.

When we experience crisis on an occasional basis, our coping skills move into full swing, helping us to adjust. After the crisis, we stop relying on those skills. That's how it should be. When crisis is chronic, however, our coping skills remain active, laying claim to our emotional resources. With much of our energy invested in coping, very little energy remains to invest in learning to live. So, we become good at one thing, surviving.

2.) Bonding. When we experience repeated crises in our lives, we become involved in a type of negative bonding. The emotional upheaval in crisis is highly emotionally charged, and if we're around it enough we bond to it. Compared to a crisis-oriented life, a non-crisis-oriented life seems flat and lifeless. We don't feel alive unless there is a crisis in our lives.

This strong negative bonding is one of the many reasons why abusive relationships are hard to leave. Abuse is a kind of crisis. It often calls for a full emotional investment in order to cope with it, an investment of the whole self. There's little energy left with which to leave, and furthermore, crisis often keeps us from forming outside relationships. There may be no other bond outside of the abusive relationship that can make us feel alive.

3.) Competence. If we are raised in a crisis-ridden environment, we learned how to handle it or we wouldn't be here. What we learn makes us good in a crisis and gives us a sense of control. Crisis becomes a place where we can feel good about ourselves, competent and capable. In the midst of crises, we feel better about ourselves. Yet, it's a two-edged sword.

4.) Confusion. At the same time that a crisis orientation makes us feel good about ourselves, we may also feel bad about being a part of the crisis. This causes confusion and leaves us with a feeling of uncertainty about ourselves. It also leaves us vulnerable to other such relationships, where familiar, crisis-ridden circumstances once again cause us to feel good about ourselves.

5.) Distorted perspective. If our parents are constantly at odds with one another and they are our models of a loving relationship, then we may come to feel that constant arguing is evidence of love. If we're involved in a relationship where there's constant upheaval, that upheaval may seem to be evidence of love.

What, then, do we need to do to overcome the weakness of crisis orientation?

▶ *Recognize our strengths.* We need first to recognize how much learning has gone into our crisis orientation. Then we'll discover how teachable we are. Those of us who are crisis-oriented have learned to bond, endure, lead, initiate, react, take risks, feel, motivate, elicit emotion from others, think creatively, hold our own in an argument, recognize and use nonverbal cues, control, recognize what we want, and make ourselves feel better. These can all be positive skills.

However, we've learned to do all of these things within the context of crisis, therefore all of them are geared toward crisis. It's a principle that we learn lessons, whether good or bad, through repeated exposure to something.

Now, through the same principle of repeated association, we need to learn to gear these skills toward normal life and more moderate levels of emotional intensity. This is done by repeatedly associating with people and situations that are non-crisis-oriented and insisting that within our current relationships crisis-oriented behaviors won't be tolerated.

▶ *Acknowledge our own power.* Recognize and acknowledge the extent of personal power involved in crisis orientation. A great deal of personal power has gone into developing all of the skills necessary for survival in our chaos-ridden lives. When we acknowledge this, we'll recognize how much power may be extracted from this weakness and invested in changing ourselves.

All of this power was summoned up from within us in order to cope with crisis. It didn't come from the crisis. The power belongs to us. Now we must learn to apply that power to non-crisis-oriented living. One thing that those of us who are crisis-oriented can never honestly say is that we don't have the power to change!

When Ellen applied herself toward non-crisis-oriented living she developed the strengths of bonding in healthy relationships; enduring uncomfortable, unfamiliar feelings and circumstances in order to develop a healthy life; leading, initiating, and motivating in positive and effective ways; responding instead of reacting; taking healthy risks; balancing her emotions; engaging in healthy, persuasive debate; and healthy self-control.

Companion Weaknesses

1√	6	11√	16√	21	26√	31	36	41	46√
2√	7	12√	17√	22	27√	32√	37	42√	47√
3√	8√	13√	18	23	28√	33	38√	43	48√
4√	9	14	19	24√	29	34√	39	44	49√
5	10	15	20	25	30√	35	40	45√	50√

I'm Uncomfortable When Someone Cries
Weakness: Pervasive Discomfort With Emotional Expression

We're all uncomfortable with something. Some of us are uncomfortable with earthquakes, frogs, or onion rings. Others of us feel that way about relatives or plaid. For me, it's quite simple. I'm extremely uncomfortable with structures of great height.

If I stand at the base of a tall building and look straight up, I faint. That makes for a very interesting, stop-and-go style of shopping in Manhattan. If I look down from a tall building, or across at other large structures, I become ill and have to get out of the building. This has made for some very quick business meetings at the highest levels. I never dine at restaurants with names starting with "Top of the...." I freeze on steep steps or stairways. Climbing up the steps to Seven Falls turned out to be clinging to the steps of Three Falls until my hands were pried from the railing and I crept backward down the steps. I imagine it's a hangover from having fallen off of a cliff in my earlier years. Just in case you've ever wondered, yes, gravity works! The good news, however, is that I can avoid most of these situations.

Our discomforts drive some of us. They affect us and our relationships. John struggled with a weakness of discomfort with emotional expression.

John

Today John can hold his own as he sits and talks with his wife about feelings. But that's not how it used to be. Before he dealt with his discomfort with emotional expression, John faced severe marital distress.

"There's no connection with John," Alice said, at one of our early meetings. "Emotionally he's not there. I want him to know how I feel, and I want to know how he feels. But we don't talk about feelings."

"I know how you feel!" John insisted.

"How could you possibly know?" Alice demanded. "You never ask how I feel. And when I try to tell you how I feel you tell me I shouldn't feel that way, or else you complain that I'm too sensitive! And you never talk to me about your feelings. I ask about how you feel and you tell me to stop trying to read your mind!"

"I just don't like it when you get all touchy-feely on me!" John admitted. It was clear that John was truly uncomfortable with Alice's emotional expression.

"Why is that?" I asked. "Why are you bothered by Alice talking about her feelings?"

"I don't know," he said. "There's nothing I can do about it."

"Is that what's bothering you—that you can't do anything about it?" I asked.

"I guess," he said. "I just don't understand why she gets so emotional."

One of the reasons why John couldn't figure out why he was so uncomfortable with Alice's emotional expression was that he had settled for the one answer that he did have. He knew that he could not fix her feelings. That left him feeling helpless and was a part of what was driving his frustration. It wasn't that he didn't care. It was just that he didn't know how to help.

Often, the real reasons for our weaknesses remain undiscovered because we settle for the answers we already have. In most cases, however, if we look beyond the most obvious answers we'll find others hiding beneath.

Where does this weakness of discomfort with emotional expression originate?

An emotionally repressive background (continued exposure to a background where emotions aren't shared or are seen as weak). John came from a family where emotions were not talked about and where sharing emotions was viewed as weakness. His discomfort with Alice's emotional expression wasn't the same thing as indifference. It wasn't that he didn't care. His frustration was driven higher because he did care. He was trained to have a negative view of emotions, and to conceal them, and he wasn't given the basic skills to deal with them. His background rendered him helpless to fix the situation. It's like taking a man who's been taught that board games are bad and who can't spell, entering him in a Scrabble game and telling him he has to win or his marriage is on the line. The pressure is enormous.

If we can understand this, we'll have greater compassion for those who struggle this way. Quite often their problem is less the discomfort with emotional expression than it is the lack of information about what to do with it. They feel helpless, not to mention pressured by the frustrations of those with whom they're in relationship. It's not about good guy versus bad guy. It's about having enough information to deal with the situation.

An overly emotive background. Just as in the case of an overly repressive emotional background, exposure to a consistently overly emotive environment also may lead to discomfort with emotional expression and a lack of trust in emotional expression.

An emotionally restrictive background. Not being allowed by a parent or spouse to express feelings can leave us with the same discomfort. The discomfort may be compounded by fear of repercussions.

How, then, do we overcome this weakness of discomfort with emotional expression?

▶ *Recognize and admit the problem.* We need to recognize and admit our discomfort with emotional expression. If we repeatedly become uncomfortable with emotional expression, we need to see that as a problem.

▶ *Discover.* We must look for the origins of the weakness. Where and when did the weakness begin? Was it recently? Or perhaps in childhood?

▶ *Evaluate the source.* We need to determine whether our discomfort made sense at the time of its origin, and decide whether it makes sense now. If our parents didn't communicate about feelings, it makes sense that we'd have been uncomfortable with emotional expression when we were children. Yet, does that mean that we should be uncomfortable with our feelings now? The answer is no. Furthermore, we might want to ask, is our lack of communication about feelings harming our relationships? Do we have a choice in the matter? Are we ourselves choosing to harm our relationships?

▶ *Develop a vocabulary.* We must develop a vocabulary of emotion. We can do this by making a list of all of the feeling words we know and then adding to that list every feeling word we can find in the dictionary. We must then begin to use these words accurately in our communication.

▶ *Practice communicating about emotion.* When communicating with others, we must change some of our questions from "What are you doing?" to "How are you feeling?" Then we need to follow up with, "Tell me more about how you feel." We must resist going into fix-it mode, and instead listen and become involved in the processing of emotions.

In the course of dealing with his discomfort with emotional expression, John developed strengths related to emotional connectedness. He developed comfort with emotional expression and the abilities to allow others closer emotionally, to give and receive love more deeply, to experience greater joy, to relate to more people, and to understand them better.

Companion Weaknesses

1	6	11	16	21√	26	31	36√	41	46√
2√	7	12	17√	22	27	32√	37	42√	47√
3	8	13√	18	23	28	33	38	43	48√
4	9	14√	19	24√	29	34	39	44	49√
5	10	15√	20	25	30√	35	40	45√	50√

THREE

Insecurity

We've all had moments of insecurity. We may have been nervous about that first date or about talking in front of a group. I wonder what we'd learn if nominated actors at the Academy Awards ceremony were electronically monitored for insecurity. I've certainly had my bouts with insecurity.

Probably like most of you, I was looking forward to my junior prom. My mother and I had found this really swank green satin dress and matching shoes. I was so ready to go! And then ... well, let me explain.

We lived in a town that was in the country. So, I guess you could say we lived in the country. That's important to know because things happen out in the country that don't often happen in a town or city. For example, how many deer have you seen launching themselves up and over the mall? How often does the fashion trend, in the city, turn predominately fluorescent orange during hunting season? Well, there I was in the little country town with my new green dress and new green shoes waiting in my closet for their big debut. But they weren't alone.

I'd moved, with my family, into an old house that had been abandoned for years—sort of. Apparently, there were residents living beneath my closet who'd not previously determined to make their presence known. They were skunks, your basic black with a white stripe down their backs, smelling exactly like they're supposed to—skunks!

I did everything possible to air out my beautiful green dress. I fretted and fumed over it for days. As prom night drew near, the stench of the skunks had been vastly reduced but there was still a trace of their delightful fragrance left. So, on prom night I masked the smell with Chanel No. 5. I could have used industrial strength Chanel No. 48.

My date was far too gracious to ever admit any problem whatsoever, so while I believed he knew that something was amiss, I couldn't be sure. The only indication I had that others knew anything about my problem was the slight tendency for space around us to subtly open up as we were dancing. Believe me, it wasn't because we were Fred Astaire and Ginger Rogers!

The insecurity I felt during prom week was enormous. Yet, it was transient and situational. It passed when the prom was over. For some of us, however, the feeling of insecurity isn't temporary at all. We struggle with feelings of being unprotected and helpless against numerous and relentless anxieties arising from an all-encompassing uncertainty about ourselves or about certain aspects of our lives. Those are the types of insecurities that we want to look at here.

I'm Tenaciously Self-Defensive
Weakness: Pervasively Needing to Be Right

Have you ever insisted that you were right, only to find out that you were wrong? I've done it so often that I'm beginning to wonder if it's a spiritual gift. I've been sure that I left the keys in one place only to find that I left them in another. I've been sure I'm right about driving directions I've given, only to find I've taken my friends down the wrong road. Nobody wants to be wrong. That's one of the things that drives the need to be right. Yet, the need to be right is often driven by more than just a desire to avoid being wrong. When this is the case, self-defense is frequently the result.

Defensiveness is a common thing. We all engage in it from time to time. Yet, some of us are tenaciously self-defensive. We always need to be right, and if we're cited as wrong, we become defensive. Carol is a good example of this.

Carol

Carol came to me with concerns about her ten-year-old daughter, Samantha.

"I tell her what I want her to do. She says that she'll do it and then she forgets," Carol said. "I discipline her but nothing changes."

"Does she have problems with remembering things in general?" I asked.

"No," Carol said. "She remembers what is important to her. She's just like her dad!"

"What do you mean when you say she's just like her dad?" I asked.

"He does the same thing," she said. "He has selective memory. He remembers only what he wants to remember. He remembers everything except what I ask him to do."

Underlying Carol's difficulty with her daughter was an issue with her husband. Samantha was imitating her father's behavior. The question was, why did Carol's husband say that he'd do what he was asked and then not do it? And why did Samantha do the same thing? I wanted to know if there was a common link between the two situations. There was.

Carol's husband explained to me that he'd shut down years before when he had realized that he could never win with Carol.

"It was always a debate," he said. "I don't think she ever really listened to me. Everything just had to go her way. So, I gave up, agreed with whatever she said just to get her off my back, and then did what I wanted to do."

Obviously Carol's husband had his own issues, passive aggression and anger among them. Yet there was one thing he described about both his and his daughter's relationship with his wife that they had in common. No one was allowed to be right except for Carol. The passive aggressiveness displayed by both Samantha and Carol's husband was a negative reaction to Carol's need to be right.

Where does the weakness of pervasively needing to be right originate?

Arrogance. Needing to be right is a learned way of thinking that may come from a number of different sources. Certainly arrogance breeds self-defense, but there are also many other sources of this weakness.

Modeling. Significant individuals in our lives, such as a parent, spouse, or sibling, may have modeled this type of behavior for us. If one of our parents was seen as the law of the house and not to be disagreed with, we may have succumbed to the model that one person holds the definition of what is right. This was Carol's story. Her mother was the one with the control in the family. She was right and everyone else was wrong. Carol was simply replicating what she'd learned as a child.

Security investment. We may be overly dependent on ourselves for our own security or for the security of others. When we have to rely on ourselves for our own sense of security, we'd better be right in our thinking and decision making. If we're not, our security is at risk. So, we become good at most things and begin to find our security and esteem in being right. For this reason, if someone contradicts us we feel as if our security has been threatened and we get defensive.

Affirmation deprivation. We may also suffer from a lack of consistent affirmation in our lives. When someone opposes us we feel shaken to the core. We feel that way because we're unsure of ourselves, because we haven't gotten the assurances we've needed to feel confident in ourselves.

Criticism. We may, at some point in our lives, have been the recipient of frequent criticism. If we've been repeatedly criticized, we may feel that we can't take any more. We may find ourselves uncomfortable with any disagreement or confrontation, and may fight to defend ourselves from even those things not intended to be criticisms.

Excess. During our lives we also may have received excessive affirmation. This may lead us wrongly to believe that we're always right.

So, how can we overcome the weakness of needing to be right?

▸ *Recognize.* We must first recognize our need to be right. This isn't that hard to do if we listen to those around us. They'll come right out and say things like, "Why do you always have to be right?" Furthermore, if those around us become passive aggressive or conflict-avoidant, we need to determine if our behavior is a contributing factor.

▸ *Track it down.* We need to determine the origins of our need to be right. We'll generally find that it's a learned behavior that we can change, not a personality trait. This was the case with Carol.

▸ *Change values.* We must begin to place a higher value on seeking the truth than on needing to be right.

Carol was blind to her weakness in part because others couldn't get through to her. At some point they quit trying. When she decided to listen to them she learned why they'd shut down. She decided to change. In the process she developed strengths in the area of openness in relationships, listening, respect for self and others, and patience. In time Carol learned that the feelings of others are usually more important than always being right.

Companion Weaknesses

1√	6√	11	16	21√	26√	31	36	41√	46√
2√	7	12√	17√	22√	27√	32√	37√	42√	47√
3√	8√	13√	18√	23√	28√	33	38√	43	48√
4√	9	14√	19√	24√	29	34√	39√	44	49√
5√	10	15	20	25√	30	35√	40	45√	50√

I Never Seem to Get Enough Approval
Weakness: Insatiable Need for Approval

Losing is never easy, but it happens to all of us at one time or another. We lose political campaigns, beauty pageants, bids for construction jobs, or bids for love. The experience starts early, with trying to get Mom's attention or waving our hands in class or on the playground and saying, "Pick me! Pick me!"

Some of us know how to lose and some of us don't. Those of us who are secure with ourselves can bow our heads with gentle recognition that we lost and someone else won. We can then raise our heads, salute the other guy, and move on. Not so with others of us. We're so desperate for approval that we can't risk losing or letting someone else win.

Let me introduce you to two people. Kathy is the leader of a very successful ministry. One of the things for which she is noted is her ability to encourage others. Randy heads up a very successful company that has become noted for the recognition it gives its employees. They both sound as if they have things well in hand, don't they? Well, they do, now. Yet, it wasn't always that way.

Kathy

Kathy sat listening to what the guest speaker had to say. She applauded when others did and smiled when she caught the speaker's eye. When the speaker had finished, Kathy moved to the podium, graciously thanked her, praising her presentation, and concluded the meeting. No one would have known that behind her gracious words and warm smile beat a heart smoldering with jealousy and resentment.

This wasn't a new experience for Kathy. While others on occasion might reasonably say of a speaker, "Well, I'm not sure I agreed with that particular point," Kathy, regardless of who was speaking, would customarily say, "Well, I sure didn't get anything out of that," or "Well, I've heard all of that before."

Kathy would also always find some little thing about the speaker that she'd turn to the negative and comment upon, perhaps in a humorous way. "Just remind me not to ever wear that shade of green," she might say with a chuckle, or, "I like her diamonds, but if she wore any more I'd have to get out my sunglasses!"

These subtle put-downs were methods that Kathy used to try to even the playing field. By putting others down, Kathy subtly made herself appear to be above them. She was trying to steal away some of the approval given to others, taking it for herself. She did this secretly because she knew it wasn't acceptable. She knew that if she said out loud what she really was really thinking—"No, don't give that praise to her, give it to me!"—she'd be met with disdain.

However, even though Kathy was so desperate for approval that she tried to block anyone else from getting any, she herself couldn't accept a compliment without discounting it. For this reason, no amount of praise was ever enough.

The irony here was that Kathy was a well-respected and accepted leader within her community. Only the highly discerning could've known how insecure and desperate for approval she was.

Randy

Randy had some of the same tendencies that Kathy did. He subtly put people down. He craved approval but minimized it when he got it. He used sarcasm to say things for which he didn't want to take responsibility. Yet he also did one thing more. Because of his unquenchable need for approval, Randy withheld approval and recognition from those in his own company who deserved it. His thirst for approval was starving his own staff of the encouragement they needed to make the company successful. He then resented them for not doing more, and raised his expectations of them. His complaints grew, and so did their dissatisfaction. What should've been a thriving, happy company was becoming a pit of discontent.

Randy and Kathy demonstrated many of the characteristics of

those who crave approval. These characteristics include: desperate, unending, and exhausting requests for affirmation; discomfort with others being approved of; jealousy; competitiveness for approval; preemptive emotional strikes; fake indifference; lying; a façade of arrogance; emotional retaliation; people pleasing; manipulation; blame; exhaustive inquisitions; emotional vacillation; and punitive behaviors. These characteristics give us a picture of how incredibly destructive the weakness of insatiable need for approval can be.

Where does this weakness of an insatiable need for approval originate?

Deficit. We may have suffered from a lack of approval at some point in our lives. Those of us who are in need of the approval and acceptance that we didn't receive in the early years of our childhood may demonstrate a need for approval that never seems to be satisfied.

When approval needs are not met in childhood, this becomes a developmental issue. Every child goes through developmental stages where the meeting of certain needs is essential to healthy development. The child sees these needs as required for survival and will go to great lengths to be sure they're met. If these needs aren't met, the child will go on to the next developmental stage with an emotional deficit, an unfulfilled need, and will then look to others to fill it. He or she will now seek to be approved of by almost everyone.

Those of us who suffer from an unmet need for approval as children are extremely uncomfortable with others' disapproval. We're continually trying to get others to fill a need that only our parents could fill. In the process, we do our best to convert others into what we need them to be, and we fail to see them and accept them for who they are. We see them as disappointments as they fail to meet needs that are impossible to meet.

Excess. Others of us may have received excessive or unwarranted approval. Perhaps we got so much approval that we began to doubt its validity or expected it to be never-ending. Either way, our need for approval in childhood was not met satisfactorily, and because of that we have continued to seek approval. How can we overcome this weakness?

▶ *Recognize.* We must recognize our insatiable need for approval, and realize that though we frequently request validation or approval, it never seems to last. We also need to acknowledge our discomfort with others' disapproval and recognize our tendency to discount compliments given to us. We must recognize any discomfort we feel when others are praised.

▶ *Challenge.* We then must challenge whether this is a need or a want. In doing this, the question we must answer is, "What will happen to me if I don't have everyone's approval?" If the answer is that we'll die, then the desire for approval is a need, because without it we wouldn't survive. If, however, the answer is that we'll be uncomfortable, disappointed, or hurt, the desire for approval is only a want, and we can live without it.

▶ *Change thinking.* We need to begin to think in terms of wants instead of needs. Wanting is an option. Need is not. If we begin to focus on wanting approval rather than needing it, we'll be less inclined to demand it, and will be satisfied with less of it.

▶ *Give it away.* We need to learn to give our approval away, and to recognize that we'll never run out. Approving of others doesn't rob us of what is ours. We aren't diminished by it. We're encouraged by it. When we hoard it we make it more precious than it is supposed to be.

▶ *Safeguard.* We must also safeguard our thoughts, and conform them to what is right. As a general rule, we should never say silently what we're not willing to say out loud, whether about someone else or about ourselves.

Both Kathy and Randy came from backgrounds where their needs for approval weren't met. Their desperation for that approval made them unhappy, and caused them to dislike themselves.

When they finally recognized what was happening, they felt relieved to know that they weren't the only ones who struggled this way. They were also relieved to discover that this was not a personality problem, but rather a problem with the choices they were making in the way that they thought about themselves.

Once they understood that their desire for approval was a want and not a need, the underlying desperation diminished and eventually left altogether. They developed strength in the area of truth. Both of them found that when they gave away their own approval instead of yielding to the weakness of an insatiable need for approval, they felt free. Ironically, when they gave their approval away, they finally began to approve of themselves. They also developed strengths in the area of giving of themselves, which inadvertently brought them the approval they no longer needed as much.

Companion Weaknesses

1√	6√	11√	16	21√	26√	31√	36	41√	46√
2√	7	12	17√	22√	27√	32√	37√	42√	47√
3	8√	13√	18√	23√	28√	33√	38√	43√	48√
4√	9	14√	19√	24√	29√	34√	39√	44	49√
5√	10	15√	20	25√	30√	35	40√	45	50√

I Have to Have Control
Weakness: Tendency Toward Being Controlling

Recently, a tiny lizard made its way into my garage and I saw it just as I was getting into my car. I stopped and watched it as it ran under my rear tire. Concerned that I might run the little lizard over, I got down on the ground and tried to make him move away from the tire. My best friend Beverly was there with me, sharing my fascination with the little fella, so I asked her to stand behind the car and make sure I didn't run him over. Once I'd pulled out of the garage, I noticed the little lizard going deeper into the garage. Concerned that he'd get trapped in the garage and be unable to get out, I tried to catch him to put him in the yard where the juicy bugs were. Unfortunately, when I tried to corral him, he darted underneath my descending hand and without meaning to I killed the poor little guy. I felt so bad that I cried. My precious friend Beverly waited a reasonable amount of time and then said what she had been fighting to keep from coming out: "Please remind me never to ask you for help!"

It felt so strange and sad to try so hard to help the little lizard, and by doing so, cause him grievous harm. If I hadn't tried to control him and his environment, he would've lived longer. Unfortunately, control, even benevolent control, is most often harmful.

Caroline is an example of this.

Caroline

"She'll ask me if I want coffee and I'll tell her I don't want any. The next thing I know, a cup of coffee will be sitting on the table right next to me," James said. "She takes the kids to soccer so I won't have to take them, but I wouldn't have them in soccer anyway. Then she gets mad if I don't do work around the house when she's with the kids at soccer!"

"I only do it for you!" Caroline responded.

The truth was that Caroline was doing these things for herself and claiming that she was doing them for James. James didn't want these things done. Caroline, on the other hand, did these things and then expected James to reciprocate. Essentially she was trying to control James by doing what she considered to be generous and kind things. Yet, kind and generous things are often seen that way only through the eyes of the one doing them. Furthermore, those things, because they are unnegotiated, don't carry with them any reasonable expectation of reciprocation or appreciation.

Caroline's method of control is just one of many. Let's take a look at some of these types.

Benevolent control. Caroline fits into this category. There are various forms of benevolent control, each exacting their own repercussions. People-pleasing is the more gentle form of benevolent control.

We don't tend to think of people-pleasing as a controlling behavior, but it is. Most of us who see ourselves as people pleasers would be uncomfortable with being seen as controlling. We see ourselves only as being helpful and nice, and we are. Yet, perhaps without knowing it at times, we control by helping.

We help in order to control our environment. We may clean up a room, saying that it was the nice thing to do, but we do it because we can't stand the mess. We may make someone go to the doctor when he or she doesn't want to go. We tell that person that it's because we love him or her, but we do it because we can't stand to watch that person be sick. We do it because we're uncomfortable with others' discomfort. We relieve our own discomfort by relieving someone else's. In the end, however, we may help to such a degree that others are robbed of the opportunity to learn from their own decisions, successes, and mistakes.

As people pleasers we may also give to people or help people in order to avoid rejection or to gain their approval or friendship. We passively manipulate them in order to get what we want. We try to play it safe by gaining a relationship indirectly, without exposing our motives. Yet the motives are the problem.

Some of us give things as a means of controlling. We give with visible or invisible strings attached. We take something wonderful and hide our motives behind it. We may even hide our motives from ourselves. We try to buy love, approval, and power, and in so doing reveal how very low is our respect for ourselves and for those we try to control.

Benevolent control leaves disappointment, anger, and confusion in its wake. At its core it's dishonest, and at its best it's disrespectful.

Aggressive control. Some of us are obvious, aggressive controllers who insist that things be done our way or else! Our mandates and accompanying intimidation occur with such frequency that those around us live in a constant state of threat. They walk on eggshells, motivated by fear of repercussions, and in doing so reinforce our controlling behavior.

This is a form of hostile control where our messages are given either directly or indirectly and are perceived as threatening: "I'm going to hit you if you do that again"; "If you don't do this you're going to wish you had!"; or "I'd advise you to pick that up." Included in the first statement is the exact harm promised. In the next two statements, the threat is implied but equally clear.

This type of control is a violation of human dignity, shattering the souls of those we love. Here, among other things, we destroy their trust and their sense of security, and distort their very sense of who they are. Even if we don't act on our threats, this is a crime.

Guilty Control. Those of us in this category of controllers see ourselves as martyrs or victims. We want others to feel bad about how they're treating us, so we pout or act like victims. We want others to feel guilty so that they'll conform to our wishes. We use guilt as the motivator. Here, we're violating the hearts of those we love.

Passive Control. The more obvious ways of passively controlling are the uses of silence and withdrawal. Yet, dependency is a more subtle one.

Some of us just won't make decisions on our own. We relinquish our ground and then hold the other person responsible for what happens with it. We come in the door and ask, "Where do you want to go to eat?" instead of expressing our own ideas about where to go. Then we get frustrated if we don't like the other person's choice. We say, "Yes, I want to, but I need to ask my spouse first." We get others to make the decisions and then we're not responsible for anything. Whatever happens, we end up looking like the good guys and the other person looks like the bad guy. Here we never have to accept responsibility. We don't have to grow up.

Assertive Control. Some of us control by trying to get others to do what we think is best for them. This is a role that parents can slip into without knowing they're doing it. What's the difference between parenting and assertive control? Parenting seeks to guide and protect while encouraging growing autonomy. Assertive control continues to make decisions for children in the place of growth toward autonomy. Parenting encourages individual development. Assertive control encourages dependency.

Those of us who are assertive controllers seem most often to be speaking in the forms of instructions or commands. Do this. Don't do that. We issue so many instructions that others don't have to do much thinking or planning for themselves. They may become resentfully dependent upon us and may fail to learn how to handle life on their own.

Assertive control in marriage is problematic because it places one person in the parent position, giving instructions, and the other in the child position. The end result will be mutual resentment and a lack of intimacy.

Persuasive or Charismatic Control. Influence and persuasion are wonderful things. We all use them, and rightfully so. In and of themselves they aren't controlling. Yet when our attempts at persuasion are relentless or the force of our charismatic personalities overwhelms those we love, violations of trust and respect have occurred.

Indirect Control. Those of us who are indirect controllers might as well be invisible. We work behind the scenes and have the school board or the church board fire that person we don't like. We just eliminate that person's position at work. We gossip and tear others down when they can't hear us. We overspend, gamble, or lie, secretly affecting those whom we love.

As controllers we present very difficult dilemmas for those whom we love. We generally don't want to control others just for the sake of control, yet we feel insecure and use controlling methods to protect ourselves.

We build an environment of mixed messages. We tell those we love that we want them to be their own persons, then in the next sentence issue a plea for them to stay with us rather than going out with friends. We're caught in a bind between what our conscience demands and what our fears tell us. We know we shouldn't control, yet if we don't we fear we may lose someone or something important to us. We feel guilty and must justify or rationalize our behavior or blame someone else. Others can't convince us of the harm we do because we can't be reasoned with. Our explanations are always too good to be defeated. We leave those we love with feelings of helplessness and hopelessness.

What are the origins of this weakness of being controlling?

Insecurity. Many of us who control are insecure. That's why there are so many inconspicuous, nonaggressive forms of control. We're so insecure that we try to control others without their knowing it. That way we don't risk rejection.

Powerlessness. Some of us who are controlling have an underlying sense of powerlessness, and we control in order to feel powerful. Arrogance is often a front for this kind of powerlessness.

Fear. Others of us control as a way of calming our fears. We control those whom we fear will leave us. We control those whom we fear will reject us. We control in order to protect ourselves from what we fear.

Selfishness. Some of us control for gain or simply because we can.

So, how can we overcome this weakness?

▶ *Look for the payoff.* We need to determine what we're getting from the control. Do we feel more secure when we have control? Then security may be what we're after. Do we feel more powerful? Perhaps we seek power. If we can determine what it is that's driving our need to control, then we can work to meet that need in healthier ways.

▶ *Determine propriety.* We then must decide if what we're getting out of our controlling behavior is a proper thing. If it is then we need to find some other means than control to get it. Remember, though, if it isn't honest, it isn't right. If it's not a right thing, then we must question why we want that thing in the first place and resolve this issue separately.

▶ *Test our motives.* We should never do anything we aren't willing to admit to out loud. Notice how our motives would be exposed: "Here, let me give you this gift so that you'll like me and won't reject me." "Let me pick you up from work so I'll know you're not with someone else." "Let me do that ugly job for you so you'll owe me." "Let me buy that thing for you because in my heart I know it's what keeps you holding on to me." We must insist upon giving and helping only in ways that do not diminish either ourselves or others.

Caroline took the emotional energy that she'd been investing in being controlling and invested it in honest self-evaluation and change. She carefully monitored her motives and conformed them to what was right and then acted on them. In doing so she developed the strengths of honesty and genuine compassion. She learned to give from the perspective of generosity rather than out of the need to control.

Companion Weaknesses

1√	6√	11√	16	21√	26√	31	36	41√	46√
2√	7√	12	17√	22√	27√	32√	37√	42√	47√
3√	8√	13√	18√	23√	28√	33√	38√	43	48√
4√	9	14√	19√	24√	29	34√	39√	44	49√
5√	10	15√	20	25√	30√	35	40√	45√	50√

I'm Plagued by Self-Doubt
Weakness: Relentless or Frequent Self-Doubt

Self-doubt isn't a new thing. When God told Moses to go speak to the Israelites, he protested, saying that he wasn't a good speaker.

> *Moses said to the Lord, "O Lord, I have never been eloquent, neither in the past nor since you have spoken to your servant. I am slow of speech and tongue."*
>
> EXODUS 4:10

Moses was so insecure about his language abilities that he asked God to send someone else! "*But Moses said, 'O Lord, please send someone else to do it'*" (Ex 4:13).

If Moses could doubt himself, I figure we all can! A part of what I find amazing about this story is that Moses, as in this situation, struggled with weaknesses. The irony in this and so many biblical stories is that God selects people with weaknesses to be his leaders! God actually uses the weaknesses of man to show his mighty power. Yet, it's only when we acknowledge our weaknesses that we can then turn to God, who will turn them to strengths.

In my practice as a marriage and family therapist, I've seen a lot of people who've struggled with self-doubt. It's kind of an equal opportunity weakness. I've seen it in corporate presidents, teachers, those in ministry, parents, children, and even athletes. In fact, this may be a good place to introduce Ted.

Ted

Ted is a baseball player. There's nothing like watching him play. He's having fun and trying to make it look like he's serious. Obviously, he's serious. This is his career and he's at the top of his game. Yet, it wasn't always this way.

At one time, baseball, for Ted, was agony. He was plagued by the weakness of relentless self-doubt. It nagged him and almost cost him his hopes and dreams.

"I can't hit anything," Ted said. "I lie there awake at night in a cold sweat, swinging and missing, swinging and missing. I don't even want to try anymore, but I have to. I've just got to do enough to stay where I am."

Ted's self-doubt never left him alone, and eventually he learned to accommodate it. He kept his expectations low so that he wouldn't disappoint himself and so he didn't have to put in the energy to perform at a higher level. He knew he was good enough to be on the team, but he didn't believe he was worthy of being there.

Leslie struggled with the same type of relentless self-doubt.

Leslie

Today Leslie confidently faces her challenges, actually looking forward to them. Yet it wasn't always that way. At one time her self-confidence was her weakness.

Leslie owned a cottage business, making and selling products at home. Orders for new products had risen enough to warrant taking the business to a higher level. As she considered the possibility of expanding, she doubted if she was equal to the task.

Leslie was lulled into sluggishness and complacency, convinced that she wasn't worthy of success, but somehow feeling that she was supposed to be successful. The emotional energy required for her to vacillate between these two ways of thinking left her without energy and motivation to succeed.

Where does this weakness of relentless self-doubt originate?

Excessively high expectations. Ted's parents were not the ones who had excessively high expectations of him. They were actually concerned that Ted's expectations of himself were far too exacting. He'd been that way for as long as they could remember. No one could tell you exactly where Ted's struggle with self-doubt came from, except that his expectations of himself were too high. What was more important than where the problem came from, however, was whether or not he could fix this. And, yes, he could.

Others of us, like Leslie, have suffered from excessively high parental expectations or perceived parental expectations. If we don't meet these expectations, we may doubt ourselves and feel that there's something wrong with us.

Lack of experience in taking responsibility. Those of us who were raised by an overprotective parent or a controlling parent who made all of our decisions for us may lack confidence in our ability to make decisions. We may doubt our own conclusions and seek continual assurances for the decisions we make. When we effusively seek those approvals we draw others into the role of parents and we fail to develop confidence in ourselves. Instead, we develop a dependency that's destined to become hostile.

Traumatic environments. Some of us had parents struggling with alcoholism, mental illness, domestic violence, or other difficulties. If we approach our mothers and ask "Mommy, is something wrong?" and she, through her tears and agony, says, "No, Dear, everything is just fine," we may became confused about our perceptions.

Unlike feelings of inferiority, which result from comparisons, insecurity and self-doubt have to do with an underlying sense of vulnerability. For this reason, insecurity and self-doubt are not likely to be resolved with encouragement based on comparisons. No matter how many times we hear, "You're just as good at that as John," the feelings of insecurity and self-doubt remain.

We may feel a gnawing sense within ourselves of something wrong with us. This isn't a sense that something is wrong, but a sense that something is wrong *with us*. We may feel depressed, as if a dark cloud hovers over our soul. We may begin to ask ourselves, "What's wrong with me? What did I do wrong?"

When we become mired in the pain of self-doubt, our minds flood with fears of rejection and loss. Yet underneath that pain resides the brightest hope, waiting to be exposed, and with its exposure the self-doubt and pain will vanish like early morning fog at the sun's rising.

So, how do we overcome self-doubt?

▶ *Answer the Question.* Never let an internal question go unanswered. Like Ted, we may struggle with painful questions: "What's wrong with me?" "Why can't I ever get it right?" We must answer these questions: "The only thing wrong with me is that I doubt myself!" "I do get it right most of the time, but like everyone else on the planet, I won't always get it right. That's normal and it's OK."

If we don't answer these questions they'll turn into self-accusations with which we'll undermine ourselves and our success. These unanswered questions will reinforce our self-doubt. In particular we must always answer "what if" questions. If the question is, "What if I don't get it right?" the answer should be, "I'll learn from this experience and get better at it." If the question is, "What if I fail?" the answer should be, "I'll get up and try again."

Answering the self-doubting questions that we ask ourselves actually prepares us to deal with the things we fear. We then feel more assured of ourselves and doubt ourselves less.

▶ *Tell the truth.* Whether or not we know the source of our self-doubt, we must always tell the whole truth about ourselves. Self-doubt is generally built on only a part of the truth, not the entirety. For example, if we think "I'm a failure!" that's only a part of the truth. We must realize that while we may have failed at this one thing, the whole truth is that we've succeeded at many things, and that we should see ourselves overall as a success.

Once Ted and Leslie began to do the work of answering their internal questions and telling the whole truth about themselves, they began to relinquish their weaknesses of self-doubt and to develop strengths of honesty and accurate self-appraisal.

Companion Weaknesses

1√	6√	11√	16	21√	26	31√	36√	41√	46
2√	7√	12√	17	22√	27	32√	37	42	47
3√	8√	13√	18	23	28√	33√	38√	43	48
4√	9√	14	19	24	29	34√	39√	44√	49
5√	10	15√	20√	25	30√	35√	40	45	50√

It's Always the Other Guy's Fault
Weakness: The Tendency to Not Take Responsibility

It starts young. Two kids are playing and one gets hurt.

"Mom!" cries one. "He hit me!"

The other kid presents his own case almost immediately.

"No, I didn't! He hit me! I didn't do it, Mom!"

The battle for responsibility goes back and forth until Mom calls an end to it, still not knowing who was to blame. Why do we blame each other? We do it because there's something at stake if we take responsibility. Pam and Richard are a good example.

Pam and Richard

Pam and Richard are doing exceptionally well these days. Richard has taken the responsibility for leadership in the marriage, and Pam is right there beside him, sharing the responsibility. They're quite the duo in business, too. They do speaking engagements together now, both of them marketing their company. Yet it wasn't always that way.

"I don't know what's going on," Pam said. "Richard isn't telling me. I have no idea if he has plans for new projects or not. He's not saying. I ask, but he just puts me off."

It was one thing for Pam to ask Richard what his plans were, but stopping there was a rather passive approach to the problem. She left the responsibility for their mutual future in his hands. She was abdicating responsibility and placing the blame for any shortcomings on Richard. She was acting as if she wasn't responsible for anything except following Richard. Yet, marriage and business require mutual responsibility for their success.

On the other hand, Richard wasn't being responsible about moving the projects forward or working closely with Pam. He blamed the stalling of the business on her, saying that he was actually avoiding her because "Pam has become a nag."

What are the origins of this weakness of not taking responsibility?

Lack of development. If we were raised in such a way that someone else always took responsibility for us, making our decisions, covering for our mistakes, we may be unfamiliar with taking responsibility and may have been taught to blame.

Fear of repercussions. If we've been exposed to an environment where there were harsh punishments for not getting things done or for doing things wrong, we may avoid taking responsibility in order to avoid those repercussions.

Avoidance. We may also lay the responsibility for what we do or what we should do on someone else because we don't want to do the work.

Fear of failure or success. We may actually fear failure or success, and may thus avoid taking responsibility for any action that could lead to these outcomes. Pam and Richard experienced this, as they were both tired of working but didn't want the company to flounder. They blamed each other for that failure. Yet they didn't want to take on the responsibility of any more success, either. So, they both pulled back, and each blamed the other for that, too.

Fear, however, wasn't the main culprit in Pam and Richard's situation. The difficulty had more to do with how they'd constructed their business relationship.

Flawed design of responsibility. The interesting thing about responsibility is that if someone abdicates responsibility, a vacuum is created. That vacuum will pull someone else into the position of responsibility, if not by taking on the task then by complaining about the abdicator. Someone either becomes a nag or takes on a role that isn't theirs. Either way, the abdication of responsibility is a weakness that is notorious for destabilizing relationships and destroying what could've been successful businesses.

Pam and Richard are in a position that is becoming more and more common today. They're not only married, they're in business together. This is a complicated situation, and susceptible to flawed designs regarding the roles of responsibility. Here's why.

When spouses are in business together they have a tendency to think that each of them is half responsible for the success or failure of the business. This sets up a dependency that eventually may become hostile. It's a potential breeding ground for blame.

There is the tendency in this arrangement to compensate for each others' weaknesses. In this case, Richard was excellent at sales but reluctant to get personally involved with people. Pam was excellent at the social aspect of the business but didn't want to learn the details of the business. So they each learned to count on the other and to cover for the other's weaknesses. Yet that's most often a setup for a failure of great magnitude.

If one of the spouses pulls back, the business suffers and so does the marriage. That's exactly what was happening in this case. Richard was tired of the sales and he was pulling back from his responsibilities. This created a vacuum of responsibility. Pam was pulled into that vacuum, but because she didn't know the details of the business, she couldn't take on the task. Instead, she took on the role of complainer.

Because they were the leaders and owners of the company, while out among the company staff, they pretended that things were great between them and with the business. Yet things weren't going well in either area. Deterioration set in and blame escalated. Eventually they blamed each other for the decline of their business.

To top it off, since they were in business together, most of their friends were business-related. Now their whole world was in trouble. They not only had to pretend that things were fine when they were with their company's staff, they also had to pretend when they were with their friends. Instead, they pulled back from their friends and compounded their problems with isolation and a lack of accountability. Things weren't looking good.

So, how can we overcome the weakness of avoiding responsibility?

▶ *Recognize the weakness.* We first need to look closely at ourselves and see if we tend to blame others for our faults. Do we avoid responsibility by passing it on to someone else?

▶ *Determine its origins.* We then need to understand what encourages this weakness. Are we afraid of negative repercussions? What are they? Loss of friendship? Loss of a job? Financial reversal? Are we concerned about our image, or about reprisal?

▶ *Consider the results.* We must then look at the long-term results of placing blame and avoiding responsibility. They will likely include broken relationships, failure to grow, and forfeiture of well-rounded success.

▶ *Review and reaffirm.* We need to review and reaffirm our values. Are the repercussions we are trying to avoid worth compromising our character? We must never sacrifice character for image or any form of safety, including emotional safety.

▶ *Accept responsibility.* We must take full responsibility for our own failures or successes. If we are spouses in business together, like Pam and Richard, we need, as individuals, to determine to be successful on our own. That way we'll end up with twice the success! Furthermore, if there are problems, we can fall back upon one another. Thinking we're half of the formula for success breeds fear of failure, because we have become dependent on someone else for his or her half of the success.

▶ *Don't compensate.* Compensating or covering for our own or some-one else's weaknesses destroys opportunity for growth. If we're in busi-ness with our spouses, or even in our marriage relationships, we must not compensate for our own or our spouse's weaknesses. If we do, we'll rob ourselves of opportunities to grow and we'll foster a hostile dependency between us. The more we cover for one another, the less we learn to handle things ourselves and the more dependent we become. We then lose our right to complain when we pull back and they don't pick up the slack, because we've set our spouse up for inad-equacy. It's better to have two fully-equipped people taking the busi-ness forward than to have two half-equipped people each waiting for the other to do his or her part.

▶ *Hold on to convictions.* The bottom line is that if we believe in what we have to offer people, we have the personal responsibility to offer it to them. This is not about somebody else. It's about us. If our spouse is afraid of success, that doesn't mean that we have to be. Yet we can't wait on him or her for our success.

▶ *Don't abdicate.* No one else can be responsible for our success. It belongs to those of us who go out and get it! We need to pursue the success that belongs to each of us, side by side, encouraging each other and helping each other along the way.

Pam and Richard took the energy they were investing in blame and avoiding responsibility and instead invested it in learning about their relationship and how to improve it. They saw that the way they had structured responsibility in the business didn't allow for or encourage maximum growth in each individual. It left room for the abdication of responsibility and for blame. They determined instead to do what was right and responsible for themselves as individuals, no matter what the other one did. They developed strengths of individual character, authenticity, courage, and genuine respect for each other.

Companion Weaknesses

1√	6√	11√	16	21√	26√	31√	36	41	46√
2√	7√	12√	17	22	27√	32√	37	42	47√
3√	8√	13√	18√	23	28√	33	38√	43	48√
4√	9	14√	19√	24√	29	34√	39√	44	49√
5√	10	15	20√	25√	30	35√	40√	45√	50√

FOUR

Anger

Early one morning, I opened the curtains on my apartment window, several stories up, only to be surprised by a window washer on a scaffolding staring directly into my face. I was so shocked that I screamed, slammed the curtains shut, and then in anger and indignation yelled at him, "Well, I hope you enjoyed that!" I then stood there for a while, in the dark, completely humiliated, and feeling like an absolute lunatic.

Many things crossed my mind as I stood there and began to calm down. What had happened to the guy on the scaffolding? Did my screaming disturb him and cause him to plummet and become a splat, a window washer statistic? Did I so frighten him that he moved on to another career?

Because I didn't want to look out of the window and check it out, I landed on a probability. I figured that, as window washers must often do, he'd probably laughed his brains out, told all of his cohorts about it at lunch, and moved on.

Here was a situation in which no one had done anything wrong, but for just a moment rage ruled. Most anger-producing situations, however, aren't so simple.

I Fight When Something Is Unfair
Weakness: Inappropriate, Excessive, or Extreme Responses to Something Unfair

While my little sister and I were walking home from school one day, a local bully rushed up to her and knocked her books out of her hands. I told him to leave her alone and he shot some crude and threatening comment back at me. I told him that if he tried anything he'd have to go through me. I was walking that fine line between brave and stupid.

He started in the direction of my sister, so I hauled off and hit him in the chest as hard as I could. The punch I landed on the bully had all of the power and stealth of an attack gnat, unlike the return punch from him, which eliminated any questions I had about whether or not people actually get hurt in fights. It hurt so much that I quickly formed the opinion that fighting is not such a stellar idea after all.

I don't like it when someone picks on the underdog or treats someone unfairly. I'm not alone in that frame of mind. Yet some of us have inappropriate, excessive, or extreme responses to something that is unfair. Jack is a good example.

Jack

Jack is an attorney. He's just the person you would want representing you if you were having difficulty. He's quick, decisive, and levelheaded, all at the same time. Yet, it wasn't always that way. There was a time when Jack responded inappropriately and extremely to unfair situations.

Jack's reputation preceded him to my office. He was and is still well regarded in the legal community. He had a reputation for fairness and ferocity in representing his clients. He came to see me with serious concerns about a recent incident that had occurred while he was visiting his relatives on the East Coast.

"My brother and I were on a ski weekend with our wives," he explained. "As we were skiing, another skier came very close to hitting my wife's leg, and I went berserk. I chased him down the hill and cut him off, making him fall. When he got up, I just punched him out!"

"What do you mean you 'punched him out'?" I asked.

"Well," he said, "this guy was screaming at me and waving his arms all around so I grabbed him, and hit him."

I listened to Jack, and the account of his behavior seemed terribly inconsistent with the man sitting in front of me. The other man wasn't seriously injured and didn't seek any medical attention. Jack wasn't worried so much about the legal ramifications of what he had done. He was more concerned about the reasons for his behavior.

"I don't understand why I did it," he said. "I just can't figure it out."

"Did you think that your wife was at risk when he came so close to her?" I asked.

"That's the interesting thing," he said. "I didn't think she was going to get hit or anything. I just thought it was so disrespectful. I can't think of a better word for it. There was my wife, a beautiful, innocent woman, clearly defenseless against this guy! I guess I felt like I needed to defend her."

"From what?" I asked. "You've already said that you didn't think she was in danger."

"I don't know," he said.

I thought back over what Jack had said and realized that his description of the circumstance suggested he felt that the situation was unfair. He mentioned an innocent woman, defenseless against a guy. This clearly paralleled his career, defending the little guy against the injustices of the big guys. Now we had a theme that extended beyond that one incident to other areas of his life. A look back into Jack's life gave us the answer we were looking for.

What's the origin of the weakness of inappropriate, excessive, or extreme responses to something unfair?

A history of being treated unfairly or witnessing unfair treatment. This was the case with Jack. Jack had been adopted along with several other children into a family where the rules and discipline were severe. His adoptive father was a tyrant who, for the slightest infraction of a rule, punished the children with angry and excessively harsh spankings. The children would be locked in their rooms until the father would let them out. Jack, the oldest child, felt guilty about not being able to help his siblings.

When Jack left home at seventeen, he swore that he'd never let anyone treat him or those he loved that way again. His whole life was eventually devoted to protecting the innocent and insuring justice for those who had been wronged. Yet, none of Jack's efforts on behalf of those treated unfairly rid him of his underlying anger at his father. It was that reservoir of anger that was tapped when Jack saw his wife pitted against the skier. His enraged response was an indication of his traumatic bond to the issue of fairness. His response was excessive, extreme, and inappropriate.

A rigid sense of justice. Jack's anger was even further aggravated because he had been conditioned to expect himself and others to live according to the letter of the law, as he'd had to do when he was young.

So, how do we overcome the weakness of excessive response to unfairness?

▶ *Disengage and gain objectivity.* We need to separate ourselves from the issue. Remember that we can become fused to the issue through trauma. We need to establish our identities based on who we are, not upon what we're fighting against.

▶ *Identify and resolve the underlying issue.* Jack's career in law, even though successful, was a way of holding a grudge. Every case he fought was rooted in his determination to restore fairness to an unfair world. He was still fighting his father. By making this connection and identifying his underlying motives, Jack was able to see the enormous effect his father had had on him.

Jack's weaknesses of excessive reactivity to the unfairness in the world led him to question himself and his own behavior. His search for understanding led him to understand that his weakness was hiding beneath the guise of a strength. He was using the justice system, and his career as an attorney, to validate the claim of his father's unfairness and to prove that he was safe from any further unfairness from his father. By defending others he was defending himself. He was saying over and over to his father, "You were wrong! What you did to me was unfair."

Jack's anger began to diminish as he talked about his relationship with his father. He took the anger stored deep within himself and externalized it by talking about it. The reservoir of rage was depleted. He chose to forgive his father, and that opened up the spiritual area of his life to growth and development. His emotional and intellectual energy began to be less invested in fighting the unfairness in the world and more invested in caring about people who had been hurt and representing them well.

As Jack extracted his emotional energy from the weakness of reactivity to things unfair, he invested that energy in enjoying the spirit of life, not just the letter of the law. He developed strengths of forgiveness, compassion, understanding, and hope, all of which brought him more success than he'd ever had before.

Companion Weaknesses

1	6√	11√	16	21√	26	31	36	41	46
2	7	12	17√	22	27	32	37	42	47√
3	8√	13√	18√	23√	28√	33	38√	43	48
4√	9	14	19√	24	29	34	39	44	49
5	10	15	20	25	30	35	40	45√	50√

I Get Angry Quickly and Over Little Things
Weakness: Quickness to Anger and Rage

There was a teacher in my high school with a penchant for throwing erasers when he got mad. Fortunately, an eraser never came my way, but I did see them in flight, and I did see the residual white chalk lines on the heads and shoulders of a few students.

It didn't take much to set this guy off. He seemed to be constantly on edge. He was particularly offended by chatting during class, so I made it a point to sit on the quiet side of the classroom. I didn't want my hair parted without my consent!

I found it interesting that eventually his anger made him vulnerable to the students' control. They'd deliberately annoy him and then enjoy the thrill of ducking to avoid the flying projectile. His very means of trying to achieve control set him up to be controlled by others.

We all get angry at times. That's normal. Yet getting angry quickly and getting angry about little things is another story. Ben is a good example.

Ben

Ben came to therapy with Sarah, his wife. She was complaining that she didn't feel that she measured up to Ben's expectations. She said that he seemed to get angry with her over every little thing. She left the trash can in the garage and he got mad. She forgot to go by the post office and he got mad. She asked him to go with her to her parents' anniversary party and he got mad. Furthermore, it wasn't just with her. He was behaving this way with the kids, too. He just seemed to be stressed out about everything.

Where does the weakness of quickness to anger originate?

Reaction to extended stress. When we're subjected to stress over long periods of time, we begin to wear down, and anger shows up. Anger is a protective emotion, and when we feel that we're at risk, anger stays closer to the surface, more readily accessible.

Repression of feelings. Anger can result when we experience frustration over a series of things but for some reason don't express or externalize that frustration. We stuff it. We know that the frustration is there, but we push it to the back of our minds and carry on. Over time, our internal reservoir of frustration and anger begins to bubble to the surface and attach itself to any little thing. At that point, our anger isn't just about the current thing, it's an accumulated emotion that can no longer be held at bay. Repression of feelings was the source of Ben's anger. For months he'd been angry with Sarah. After a failed attempt to address the root issue with her, he didn't want to try again. So he stuffed his anger inside and eventually it started attaching itself to every little thing.

Perfectionism. When we're under the mistaken notion that things can be perfect, we get upset if they aren't. Part of the anger here comes from the fact that the perfectionist is the one who holds the definition of how things should be. We base our expectations of others on our own standards. Because the standards are ours and not those negotiated with or agreed to by others, they don't meet them, and we're constantly disappointed. Furthermore, perfectionism is vastly detail-oriented. Each detail becomes a part of an expectation where disappointment occurs. The more details there are, the more disappointment there'll be. The more anger there is, the more easily we become angry.

Control. We want things our way. We've somehow convinced ourselves that others should do what we say. If they don't, we see their behavior as disrespectful and we're angered quickly and over every point of disrespect. Sometimes we use our anger as a motivator to get something done. Sometimes, however, our controlling anger is diversionary. We use it to keep people confused, doubting themselves, and dependent on us.

Defensiveness. When we're insecure or afraid, we may send our feelings into hiding, but anger is the one emotion that remains available to defend and protect us. It's a kind of guardian. That is a part of why those of us with troubled pasts are frequently angry. Guardian anger not only remains to protect the rest of our feelings, but since it is the only emotion that is easily accessible, it serves as the "emotion for all seasons." All other emotions are filtered through this anger. We may yell at someone to indicate concern. We may scold to indicate appreciation.

This causes confusion in the minds of those we love. They sense that we love them but because we present that love cloaked in anger, it's unsafe for them. This is a powerful mixed message. People get addicted to it. They tolerate the bad in order to hold on to the good. This is one reason why it's difficult to leave abusive relationships. There is a mistaken notion that abusive individuals don't really love those whom they abuse. This isn't always true. They often do, even though they treat people horribly. It's the existence of that love in the midst of hateful behavior that keeps people hanging on. It's important to understand this or we'll see abusers as unredeemable and the abused as completely out of touch with truth.

How do we overcome the weakness of quickness to anger?

▶ *Determine the reason for our anger.* We need to answer the following questions: "What was the payoff for my anger? What happened after I expressed my anger? What did I get out of expressing my anger?" Most often when we find the result of the anger we've found its reason. Did we achieve the control for which we were looking? Did we hurt someone? Did we get emotional relief for a few moments, intimidate someone, or protect ourselves?

▶ *Challenge the acceptability of the result.* We need to ask ourselves whether what we got out of our anger was right and good for everyone involved.

▶ *Challenge the acceptability of the method.* If the result of our anger is acceptable, then we need to ask ourselves whether anger was an appropriate method for reaching this result.

▶ *Take appropriate action.* If what we were after was a good thing, then we must find another method of achieving the desired result. If it was a wrong thing, we need to deal with why we were after that thing.

Companion Weaknesses

1√	6√	11√	16√	21√	26√	31	36	41√	46√
2√	7	12√	17	22	27√	32√	37	42	47√
3√	8√	13√	18√	23	28√	33√	38√	43	48√
4√	9√	14√	19√	24√	29	34√	39√	44	49√
5√	10	15√	20	25√	30√	35	40√	45√	50√

People Don't Meet My Standards
Weakness: Subscribing to Excessively High or Unnegotiated Expectations

We all have expectations. I'm not supposed to hit you, and you're not supposed to hit me. We haven't talked about it or negotiated it personally, but we share that expectation based on an understanding of mutual survival and the law. If either of us violates that expectation, we have the right to be angry and to seek some type of remedy.

Expectations are healthy things when they are negotiated, held in common, and not excessively high. Yet, there are problems with some expectations, even some negotiated ones. The anger that emerges when these expectations aren't met is inappropriate and harmful. Peter is a good example.

Peter

Today Peter has a wonderful relationship with his family. All wounds are healed and no one walks on eggshells anymore. If you encountered the family for the first time, you'd never guess that this family used to be tyrannized by the weakness of the father.

My first meeting with Peter also included his wife, Amy. Sitting out in the waiting room was Gabriel, their seventeen-year-old son, the oldest of their three children. Later I learned that Gabriel was there to protect his mother, should his father become enraged.

"I can't take it anymore," Amy started. "Nothing I do is ever good enough. I'm tired of living in fear of Peter's anger. It's affecting the kids, too. We all walk around on eggshells, scared to death that we'll do some little thing that will set him off."

They came to see me after an angry incident the night before when Peter had yelled at his ten-year-old daughter over her not understanding something in her homework assignment.

Abby ran to her room, afraid that her father was going to hit her. Unnerved, Amy could take no more. "You expect too much of us!" Amy cried. "You expect us to be perfect, and we're not!"

What are the origins of this weakness of excessively high or unnegotiated expectations?

A previous environment of high or unnegotiated expectations. Peter's expectations of how the family members should behave had for the moment become more important than the emotional safety of those family members themselves. Peter was treating his family in the same way that he'd been treated when he was a child. Excessively high expectations had been mandated by Peter's father, without any negotiation with the family and without proper consideration of family members' individual differences. Peter was simply following the modeling of his father.

Perfectionism. When we think about demanding or unattainable standards, we automatically think of perfectionism, and rightfully so. Perfectionism demands the impossible. Anger is likely to follow.

People-Pleasing. At the core of our people-pleasing behavior is an anticipated reciprocal response. We'll do this thing for you and then, without your knowing it, we'll expect that you'll like us, or not reject us, or owe us. We have an un-negotiated expectation, which, when unmet, gives rise to seething anger. Our subscription to the undisclosed and unnegotiated expectation is what causes our anger. The only way out is to be sure that our expectations are exposed and negotiated. An unnegotiated expectation doesn't rightfully contain the privileges of disappointment and healthy anger.

Repeated Behavior. When behavior is repeated over a period of time, expectations begin to form. These are unspoken and unnegotiated expectations based on the anticipation that the unbroken pattern of behavior will continue. This is a breeding ground for dependency in relationship and anger.

So, how do we overcome the weakness of excessively high or unnegotiated expectations?

▶ *Recognize and admit.* We must recognize and acknowledge that our standards are too high and are unnegotiated. If we listen, others will tell us, with words or actions, that we're expecting too much of them. Listen for complaints about what is being asked. Notice any nonverbal cues like sighing or rolling eyes. Ask for others' input about what's is being asked of them. This will take some of the fuel typically used in being angry and instead invest it in developing the strengths of listening and caring.

▶ *Track it down.* If possible, we need to track down the origins of this weakness. When we see that this is learned behavior and that it originated with someone else, we can become more objective about the issue. The weakness isn't a part of our personality for which we must fight. It's nothing more than something we've learned. It's an option, not a personality trait.

Most often we've held on to something harmful because we mistakenly think that it's a part of us and we're violating ourselves if we let it go. Yet, if we let it go, we'll find that we're still there, and in fact have been freed from our self-imposed tyrant. Now instead of using our energy to fuel the tyrant, we can use that same energy to fuel the strengths of personal freedom and development.

▶ *Negotiate rather than mandate.* Except for survival-related expectations, we must never subscribe to expectations that haven't been negotiated and agreed upon. If we can avoid doing this, we'll pull some of our energy away from making faulty assumptions and exacting excessively high expectations. We can then invest it in developing the strengths of negotiating and respecting others' opinions.

Peter was unaware that he still had a good deal of emotional energy invested in hidden resentment of and lack of forgiveness for his dad. These became areas of weakness that were then inflicted on his family. He was able to turn those weaknesses into strengths by acknowledging that they were there and determining to overcome them. He forgave his dad, which led him to become more forgiving in general. Once he had forgiven his dad, the resentment he'd been harboring was dispersed, and the energy that Peter had been investing in this resentment could be redirected into correcting the kinds of mistakes he'd learned from his dad. The weakness of excessively high and unnegotiated expectations was turned into the strengths of effective communication, closeness, and respect born out of learning to negotiate, rather than mandating.

Companion Weaknesses

1	6√	11√	16	21√	26√	31	36	41	46√
2	7	12√	17√	22√	27√	32√	37	42√	47√
3	8√	13√	18	23√	28√	33√	38√	43	48√
4	9	14√	19√	24√	29	34√	39	44	49√
5√	10	15	20	25√	30√	35√	40	45√	50√

I Get Upset If I'm Misrepresented
Weakness: Excessive Need to Be Seen Accurately

Most of us would get upset if someone kept insisting that we'd been seen on a wanted poster at the post office. Yet what if someone said we arrived at some irrelevant meeting at three o'clock even though we arrived at two o'clock? Would that matter enough to be upset about it? It would to some of us, and we'd fight to get a retraction on the comment!

Why is it that some people get so upset if they're are misunderstood or misrepresented? Perhaps David can give us some clues.

David

David came to me at the recommendation of his wife, who had begun to be concerned about him. She told me that David had become increasingly involved in his work, and increasingly inflexible and demanding in dealing with her and their children. When his friends approached this topic with David, he became angry and adamant that *he was not what he was being made out to be!* They suggested that he speak with his pastor about the issue, but David declined. They recommended that he see a therapist, but again, he declined.

Two weeks later David became enraged at his wife for a comment she'd made in front of their friends, and when they got home he screamed and yelled at her for a solid hour. Their four children were all in their rooms, shivering with fright. In the midst of his rage, his youngest daughter came into the living room where he was yelling at his wife. "Daddy, don't!" she cried. "Please, Daddy, don't!" He turned to his daughter, calmed down, and tried to comfort her. David's heart was broken over what he'd done, and it was at that point that he called me.

David had always seen himself as a strong, self-assured man, successful in business and in his marriage. It didn't surprise me that his strengths would have to begin collapsing before he'd seek help. That's a sure indication that some of those strengths were artificial; once they didn't provide the service they were intended to provide, they began to dissolve. When they did, everything they were hiding came into view. When David came to my office that's how he felt: exposed.

"Why did you do it?" I asked. "What was all that rage about?"

David sat forward in the chair across from me. He was a handsome, well-dressed, and apparently successful businessman. He gathered his thoughts before he spoke.

"Well," he said, "we were with a group of people and my wife said something that really made me mad and I just lost it." Apparently his wife had commented on his parents having been poor farmers in Iowa and David thought she shouldn't have said it.

I took a few moments to dispel David's misconception that rage was an out-of-control experience. Unfortunately, that's a common misrepresentation of the facts, even within the therapeutic community. I knew by his comments that he was upset with his wife while they were out with their friends, but he didn't let it show. He was angry in the car on the way home, but he didn't let it show because there were others in the car with them. He was angry when he put the children to bed, but he didn't let it show. So, every step of the way he had control over his rage. He wasn't out of control. He was so in control of his anger that it was laser-like. He aimed it only at his wife and only in private. It was very deliberate. Once that myth was dispelled and it was clear to David that he was responsible for his actions, we moved on.

Where does the weakness of an excessive need to be seen accurately originate?

Insecurity or an underlying sense of shame. David felt that the information about his parents should've remained private. He was embarrassed by his background, and he felt it tarnished his image of sophistication. He felt shattered, reduced to almost nothing. Because of that his response was a survival response, a combination fight-and-flight response. David had worked for years to distance himself from his parents' impoverished background. That's why he worked so hard. He thought that if he became successful then maybe he wouldn't feel like or be seen as a poor plowboy anymore.

Excessive concern about what others think. When our sense of who we are comes from how others see us, we become dependent on them for our self-esteem. We can't risk them having a misperception of us because our identity is invested in their perspective. This is a terribly vulnerable place to be, as our perceptions of ourselves and our corresponding moods are in the hands of others.

Perfectionism. If we believe that we must be perfect, then any negative perception of us will bring serious disappointment and anger.

How do we overcome the weakness of excessive need to be seen accurately?

▸ *Identify and admit the weakness.* What David saw as his strengths, in the long run turned out to be his weaknesses. His work and his image provided him a place to hide. They became diversions from the whole truth about him. They became the shield that he used to protect himself from any outside attack. Yet they also became a prison for him and for his family. They protected him from the wrong people and robbed him of his authenticity. Once he saw the role that these seeming strengths were playing in the destruction of his life, he was willing to reevaluate them and call them what they really were—weaknesses. Once his weaknesses were identified and understood, he was in a position to deal with them.

▶ *Resist and decline.* We must resist any frequent or repeated urge for self-defense. Instead, in general, we need to let our behavior speak for us. We must decline any method of self-presentation that would present us in an inauthentic light. In doing so we will drain the fuel from our weakness of excessively needing to be seen accurately and reassign it to developing strengths in the area of honesty and integrity.

▶ *Tell and live the whole truth.* David came to understand that his intense and excessive need to be seen accurately was a weakness. It presented him in a light that wasn't accurate in its entirety. It compromised his character and integrity. When he openly told the whole truth, the pressure was relieved. He no longer had a reputation to live up to. Instead, he had to face his history and deal with it. That would bring him freedom. His anger disappeared and his family finally felt that they had their husband and father back. David used the energy he'd once used to run away to get to know those he loved. He gained the strengths of honesty, integrity, and humility.

Companion Weaknesses

1√	6√	11√	16√	21√	26√	31√	36	41√	46√
2√	7	12√	17√	22	27√	32√	37	42	47√
3	8√	13√	18√	23	28√	33	38√	43	48√
4√	9	14√	19	24	29	34√	39√	44	49√
5√	10	15	20√	25√	30	35	40√	45	50√

I Hate Myself
Weakness: The Tendency Toward Self-Loathing

I remember getting up one morning and looking into the mirror. I couldn't believe what was looking back at me. I looked like a freeka-zoid. There was a red line on my face where the seam of the pillow had left its imprint, and apparently while I was sleeping a big north wind had blown in and plastered all of my hair to one side of my head. I looked like I'd been standing dangerously close to a rocket train.

Most of us have looked into the mirror at one time or another and said silently, "I hate the way I look!" Yet, usually, this is a temporary disenchantment. For others, however, that negative self-perspective grows into self-hatred and becomes a destructive weakness. For a long time, Gina strenuously held on to the weakness of self-hatred.

Gina
I haven't seen Gina for years, but I can still see her face as it was when she came to me as a nineteen-year-old. She was of medium height, slender, with gorgeous fair skin and long, beautiful, flowing auburn hair. It was the kind of color that every hairdresser wishes he or she could copy. Gina was beautiful in anyone's eyes, except hers.

I listened to Gina tell me about her struggle with anger. She described how she'd recently become so angry that she'd wanted to run her car off the side of a cliff. She hated life and she hated herself. No one would have known it by looking at her.

"What are you so angry about?" I asked.

"I hate my life," she said.

"Tell me what you hate about your life." I was somehow not sur-prised by her response.

"I hate the way I look! I hate my height. I hate my body." She waited for a startled look from me which I couldn't give her. I'd seen this too many times before.

Gina was struggling with perfectionism, and it had her at the precipice of an eating disorder. All of her money and success couldn't satisfy her need for perfection or rid her of her self-hatred. In fact, her self-hatred was indispensable to her perfectionism.

What's the origin of this weakness of self-hatred?

Negative self-appraisal based on past or current behavior. Some of us hate ourselves because we've done things wrong in our lives. This is our form of punishment, and it needs to be replaced with self-forgiveness and an acceptance of responsibility.

Negative self-appraisal based on someone else's opinion. We may hate ourselves because we've been convinced by someone else that we're worthy of being hated.

Perfectionism, excessively high expectations, or excessive criticism. Those of us who have been frequently criticized, especially as children, or who have become perfectionists have the tendency to use hostile and negative reinforcement to make ourselves "do better next time." We become self-critical not only because this was modeled for us, but also because now it has become our way of motivating ourselves. This was true of Gina.

We may enjoy the euphoria of success for a few fleeting moments or days, but then we swiftly repress the excitement of success underneath a firm determination to do better next time, and we do so with a keen eye toward what we perceive to be errors or omissions in the last effort.

Our tendency to have high expectations of ourselves, along with the modeling we may have had of criticism and the suggestion that we'll never really "measure up," all combine to place a great deal of importance on continually improving. To protect ourselves from doing less than we think we should, and to protect us from the disappointment of failure, we "hold ourselves down." We don't allow ourselves to be outwardly excited. Instead, we say to ourselves and others, "Well, I'm not sure how this is going to turn out." The negative slant on the comment causes us to always be working just a little bit harder. It also guards us against high hopes and prepares us for possible disappointment. We learn over time to use negative reinforcement to push ourselves to ever higher levels of effort.

There are problems with this approach, however. First, we can't allow ourselves to experience the joy of excellence or to demonstrate that joy authentically to others. Rather, we secretly suspect that what we've done is in fact good, but we don't want to build ourselves up. After all, we may fail, and even if we don't, we'll need to do better next time. Others say, "I'm sure you'll do well," because they know our history, but we smile hesitantly and "hold ourselves down." We've created a false image of ourselves, with false humility. Who we really are has gone underground and is busy developing a hidden inner world of self-hate. Because the use of negative reinforcement does, in fact, drive us to do better, it's addictive. We don't postpone our joy in doing well; we rob ourselves of it altogether.

So, how do we overcome this weakness of self-hatred?

▶ *Recognize its use.* Gina was afraid to let go of her self-loathing. It had become the tool that she used to keep herself thin. That's one of the many dangers of self-hatred as a motivator. It's extremely powerful, and once it goes beyond a negative self-evaluation to become a tool for success it begins to seem indispensable. We begin to rely upon it to keep ourselves on track.

▶ *Break the obsession.* Self-loathing is self-consumption. We need to look outside of ourselves and become more concerned with others than with ourselves. Once we've broken the obsessive hold that self-hatred has on us, we can then look at the situation more objectively. The emotional, physical, intellectual, and spiritual energy required for self-loathing is enormous. We must rob self-hatred of each and every particle of energy at every opportunity.

▶ *Tell the truth.* We must face the fact that we're not helpless. We don't unconditionally want help. We want approval from others but not from ourselves. We're more interested in our self-image than anything else in the world. We've secretly mistaken self-loathing for courage and truth.

▶ *Reckon with objective reality.* Is this the way we really want to be? If we say yes to any part of this question, we're deluded and purchasing tomorrow's misery in advance. We need to responsibly take every spiritual, medical, psychological, and psychiatric step available to get help. Then we need to comply with those exercises that will rid us of this obsession.

Like all of us who struggle with self-hatred, Gina was reluctant to give up this image. She struggled with depression, which required medication. Dealing with the depression first seemed to help Gina with her obsessiveness. The fact that she was responsible in that area led to her to be able to be responsible about her self-appraisal and the use of negative reinforcement. Every ounce of energy she extracted from her weakness of self-hatred she reinvested in developing the strengths of telling and living according to the truth and developing relationships. It was a long road for Gina, and she was able to conquer her weakness of self-loathing only by doing absolutely everything possible to overcome it. In doing this, Gina developed the strength of genuine courage.

Companion Weaknesses

1√	6√	11√	16√	21√	26√	31	36√	41√	46√
2√	7√	12√	17	22√	27√	32√	37	42	47√
3√	8√	13√	18√	23	28√	33√	38√	43√	48√
4√	9√	14√	19√	24	29√	34√	39√	44√	49√
5√	10√	15√	20	25	30√	35√	40√	45√	50√

FIVE

Pride

We all have our bright and shining moments. I had one. As a tiny tot I'd heard that there was going to be a kite-flying contest at a nearby park. All of the kites had to be built by children, and awards would be given for the best kites. It didn't bother me that the other kids were bigger than I. I figured that a termite was smaller than a house, but in a contest the termite would win! I decided I would be the termite of the kite kingdom.

I was just a wee little thing so I decided to make a wee little kite. It was great. I got out a cupcake paper cup and flattened it, forcing all of its little pleats to give way to my plan. Then I pressed it with the Betty Crocker cookbook. I searched the yard for sticks, with no luck. Toothpicks, pencils, and Pick-up sticks were out. Then came the solution. Popsicle sticks! In the name of science I ate the cherry ones, which left me with two near-perfect sticks. A quick chop down the middle and they were done.

I used Elmer's Glue on the sticks, tied on a string and a tiny little kite tail, and was off to the competition. Look out, Orville and Wilbur! There I was among the box kites, the parachute kites, and the painted kites with my cupcake kite. I was a proud termite! Never mind that their kites were soaring and mine was hanging down somewhere around my ankles.

If it hadn't been for that one obscure rule about kites having to fly, who knows what I might have won. As it was, I won a ribbon for the littlest kite in the competition and it might as well have been a Grammy!

There are times when it makes sense to have reasonable pride in our accomplishments. Yet, pride can become a problem. That's what we'll be talking about in this chapter.

People Always Tell Me I'm So Smart
Weakness: Mistaken Self-Perception

Chuck, my cat, was a real pal who hated my being away from him for extended periods of time. Since I don't speak cat, let me tell you how I knew that.

The first time I returned from a trip, Chuck appeared to have gotten sick while I was away. He had long, fluffy, blue-gray hair and like most cats, he was meticulous about his grooming. Yet, when I got back from my trip his fluffy hair had gone flat! It was unkempt, sickly! There were tears in his eyes and he had a scowl on his face. His bowl was full of food and he had water, so he wasn't starving. I figured he was sick.

With comfort and attention he improved. "Close call," I thought. However, I was naive to the ways of cats and unaware that I had just been fooled by a conniving, manipulative, overstuffed quadruped of the feline variety! Over time, I figured it out.

After a few more trips, leaving Chuck in expert hands, I realized that the flat hair routine was deliberate. I'd come home and greet the scowling little flat-haired fur-ball only to find that within moments the hair would fluff up like something from the fifties and the scowl would disappear. This flat hair routine was Chuck's way of expressing discontent with my being gone and his way of getting my attention. There's nothing like being a human being subject to behavior modification devised and instituted by a cat! Good grief!

In the same way that I misperceived Chuck's behavior, we're all subject to misperceptions. We misread what others say, their facial expressions, and sometimes their behaviors. At times we even misread ourselves. If such a misperception persists, it becomes a weakness jeopardizing the foundations of our true self and our relationships. This is what happened to Matt.

Matt

Matt came to me because his wife, Jean, had left him, and one of her conditions for restoration of the relationship was that he receive counseling.

"I don't have issues," he said. "I'm only here because my wife is having problems."

Matt said Jean was "just not smart enough" to deal with him on many levels.

Jean, who was clearly intelligent, an excellent communicator, and well informed, complained that Matt "tears me to pieces arguing with me. I can never win! He runs me over with words. He thinks he knows everything and I'm an idiot."

Focusing on her last comment, I asked Matt if his friends ever kidded him about knowing so much. Several had. I asked if Matt had any close friends. He didn't. I wondered if more than his marital relationship was suffering from his "know-it-all" perspective.

In reality, Matt's intelligence was probably about the same as that of his wife. Why did he insist that he was so much smarter than she was?

Where does the weakness of mistaken self-perception originate?

Over- or underdeveloped skills. In his childhood Matt was constantly "locked in verbal combat" with his mother, a college professor. Matt learned verbal warfare as a way of fighting the feeling of being "painted into a corner" by his mother. "It was the only way I could survive," he said. "It was a win or lose proposition."

To win and in his estimation to survive, Matt, the child, had to match wits with his adult parent. That exercise caused him to be more skilled in verbal debate than other children his age. That advanced verbal skill was applauded and encouraged by adults, who mistook his overdeveloped verbal skill as a sign of natural intelligence.

Hearing the accolades and mistaking his verbal skills for intelligence, Matt began to believe the misperception, seeing himself as excessively intelligent. He failed to see his advanced verbal skills as learned behavior. This, then, became his unfortunate and unwitting platform for arrogance.

When one area of our lives is overdeveloped, it is at the expense of another area, which becomes underdeveloped. While Matt's skills at verbal debate were overdeveloped, his social skills were underdeveloped.

On the flip side of the coin, others of us may misperceive ourselves because we have underdeveloped skills. As an example, if we don't communicate well, we may see ourselves as unintelligent.

Being defined by others. If we care excessively what others think about us, we may become vulnerable to taking our definition of ourselves from them. If they think we're smart, we may think we're smart. If they say we're stupid or unworthy, we will too.

So, how can the weakness of mistaken self-perception be overcome?

▶ *Challenge the perception.* In the same way that we challenge negative self-perceptions to determine if they are true, we must also challenge the positive ones.

▶ *Determine the origins of the perception.* The origins of Matt's mistaken self-perceptions began with the accolades he received for his verbal skills, equating his verbal skills with intelligence.

▶ *Determine and challenge what maintains the perception.* If the things that maintain a perception are faulty, the perception may be as well. The accolades of adults were not evidence of Matt being more intelligent than the other children. The adults didn't know whether they were looking at innate intelligence or learned behavior. Matt's peers couldn't provide a proper comparison because he didn't listen to them. In order to determine whether he was more intelligent than others, Matt would have to listen to those others. When he started listening, the first thing he heard was their complaints.

▶ *Consider what others say without being defined by those perceptions.* See if there is any truth in the specifics of what they say. Matt was given specifics about the use of his verbal skills. He finished other people's sentences, said they didn't know anything, talked over them, looked at them condescendingly, used pretentious words, switched topics to throw them off, and argued them into the ground. All of these specific complaints were true.

▶ *Correct those things that contribute to a faulty perception and what remains will be the accurate perception.* To get Matt to see what was emotionally driving him, I asked him, while in conversation with Jean, to stop at every urge to do any of the things listed in the preceding point. Then he was to admit what he'd had the urge to do and how he felt at not doing it. Here's what he found.

He finished other people's sentences because he grew impatient and angry with them for taking so long to finish. He had an unnegotiated expectation, and he became angry when this expectation wasn't met. Once he saw this, he stopped following the urge to be impatient or controlling, using the urge instead as a reminder to reroute his mental and emotional energy into being patient. The urge to finish others' sentences disappeared as the emotional energy that once fueled anger, impatience, disrespect, and control was rerouted into developing the strengths of respect, patience, and self-control.

Matt's insecurity drove him to put people down. He raised his voice and talked over those who disagreed or had better ideas. It made him feel insignificant and insecure to hear someone sound more intelligent than he did. His arrogance was a cloak for insecurity.

Matt built his sense of self on the faulty impression that he was more intelligent than others. Because his sense of self was at risk if he lost an argument, he fought to win.

When he stopped finishing others' sentences, he had to listen to others and became interested in them. He was no longer seen as arrogant, and more friendships became available to him. He began to understand that his verbal skills were overdeveloped and began to take responsibility for the harm he could do by using those skills improperly.

One more thing happened as Matt unraveled the roots of his faulty perception. As the blocks to his communication were removed he found that others had much to say and much worthy of listening to. Perhaps he wasn't smarter than all of the rest, but it didn't matter anyway. He had a full life now, complete with friends and an occasional enjoyable casual conversation. The wonderful man Matt really was began to shine through once the weakness of an inaccurate self-perception was recycled into strength of character.

Companion weaknesses would depend upon the specific misperception of self. The companion weaknesses that would commonly accompany Matt's mistaken self-perception are checked here.

Companion Weaknesses

1√	6√	11√	16	21	26√	31√	36	41√	46√
2√	7√	12√	17√	22√	27√	32√	37	42√	47√
3√	8√	13√	18√	23	28√	33√	38√	43	48√
4√	9	14√	19√	24√	29	34√	39√	44	49√
5√	10	15	20	25√	30√	35	40√	45√	50√

I Excel at Most Everything
Weakness: Excessive Self-Reliance

Do you remember back in high school or college when you were a part of a group that was given a collective assignment? Some of the group members were thrilled because it would be the first time they got an "A." Others were neither here nor there about it, and then there were the individualists and overachievers who were exceedingly put off by the idea. They knew that they were going to have to work harder to compensate for those who'd work less, and they couldn't figure out why they should be tortured so! Why should they be saddled with underachievers? The funny thing was that the exercise was often a test of cooperation. Those who were overachievers in other areas became underachievers in the area of cooperation. It's not that they don't like others; it's just that they're used to doing things themselves. Rebecca's story is a good example of this excessive self-reliance.

Rebecca

Rebecca had no trouble with communication except when it had to do with her understanding of relationships. She could tell me easily about tasks she'd performed, but except for anger she couldn't tell me much of anything about feelings. When her anger started spilling onto her children, her husband recommended she see a therapist.

Rebecca was the sharpest tack in the box. One look at her and you could tell how competent and capable she was. She oozed the stuff! Dressed to the tens, perfectly coifed, no one stood out like Rebecca. Most every woman within a visual radius of Rebecca wanted to be her! Yet, being her friend was another story.

Rebecca's friendships had the turnover rate of mid-management in America. Just in case you were wondering, that's not a good thing. Two months before she came to see me, Alice was her best friend. Not long before that it was Cynthia. When she came to see me her best friend was Cathy, but word on the street was that Cathy looked like history. What was going on? Why was Rebecca having such difficulty maintaining friendships? In a nutshell, Rebecca was so self-reliant that her friends didn't feel that she needed them.

Rebecca's friendships originated at church. She met people when they worked on projects together. When she was given the position of leadership on a project, others jumped at the chance of working with her. Not long after signing on, however, they would find that there was nothing important for them to do because Rebecca already had it covered. Rebecca had become self-reliant at the expense of learning to share responsibility, power, and praise. Those who stayed on the project usually did so in hopes of developing a friendship with Rebecca. Yet they found that her self-reliance translated into her personal life as well.

Other friends get together often to talk about what's happening in their lives. They help each other paint the house, go to movies together, and work on projects together. It didn't work that way with Rebecca. She didn't need help, so there was no need for reciprocation. Being so self-reliant, she didn't need to count on others. Had she needed them, she'd have learned to expose herself to them emotionally, to share herself with them. Unfortunately, however, her extreme self-reliance kept her out of touch with her own needs and those of others. That meant that Rebecca needed people around only when she could use them for some purpose. When that purpose was gone, there was no longer any need for those people to stay around. Why was this happening with Rebecca?

What are the origins of the weakness of excessive self-reliance?

Perfectionism. Perfectionism demands that everything be done perfectly. Because of that, the perfectionist usually works alone or follows others around and improves on what they've done. This was one of Rebecca's weaknesses.

Background of over-responsibility. If we've experienced an environment where we were assigned or we assumed excessive responsibility, we may continue to be overresponsible even after we leave that environment.

Need for control. Some of us just don't exercise patience with others. We want control over when and how things are done. We subscribe to the notion that it's easier just to do things ourselves. This was another of Rebecca's weaknesses.

Previous modeling and lack of skills development. We may have had an overly responsible parent as a model of overresponsibility. We may be over-responsible because we were never taught to share responsibility.

Fear or insecurity. Some of us are so afraid of doing something wrong that we take care of things on our own in order to avoid any scrutiny or accountability. Rebecca was in this category, too.

How can this weakness of excessive self-reliance be overcome?

▶ *Recognize the weakness.* We need to evaluate our relationships and see if we're sharing responsibility and recognition with others. If not, we may be overly self-reliant. We need to ask ourselves the following questions: Do we enjoy the successes of others? Can we join in their joy of accomplishment with them or are we too competitive? Do we keep secret things that would benefit others and use them only to our own gain?

▶ *Recognize the value of others' efforts.* We need to allow others to do some of the things that we can do, so that we can have the opportunity to appreciate them and praise them. We need to teach others what we know so that they may grow at the expense of our excessive self-reliance.

▶ *Appreciate the person more than the task.* We need to get our values straight. The task is never more important than the person. Excessive self-reliance occurs at the expense of healthy relationships.

Rebecca gradually began to release some of her responsibility and the praise that came with it. It wasn't easy, and she actually entered a process of grieving over the loss of her overachiever image. Learning to share was painful for her, but she did it and eventually she began to enjoy it. When she withdrew her emotional investment from excessive self-reliance, and after a good deal of physical rest, Rebecca began to invest in others and care for them. She developed the strengths of sacrifice, generosity, and honest, healthy relationships. She actually began to need people, and while it wasn't easy for her to be just one of the group, she did it. In doing so she developed strengths in the area of relational courage and willingness to expose her own challenges for the sake of others' growth. Now, everyone within a visual radius wants to be her friend.

Companion Weaknesses

1√	6√	11√	16	21√	26√	31	36	41√	46√
2√	7√	12√	17√	22	27√	32√	37	42√	47√
3√	8√	13√	18√	23√	28√	33√	38√	43	48√
4√	9	14	19√	24√	29	34√	39√	44	49√
5√	10	15√	20	25√	30√	35	40√	45√	50√

I Can Handle Anything!
Weakness: Tendency Toward Being Over-Responsible

I was at a party once where the decorations were incredible and the food rivaled that of any professionally catered event I'd attended. I was so impressed and so well cared for!

The woman who was throwing the party was in constant motion. I noticed that almost every time someone needed something, a coaster, food, something to drink, she was on it almost before they could make the need known. It was amazing and, as usual, I made no attempt to keep myself from turning her into the subject of my experimentation and observation. I'm sure I'll be punished for this someday!

While she was circulating among the guests, I put into play a plan of my own devising. I sat down and, with soda in hand, looked anxiously about as if in need of a coaster on which to set my drink. In a few moments a coaster mysteriously arrived. I rose and looked in all directions as if looking for the restroom, and swiftly, without my asking for them, I was given directions to rest room. It was spooky. I wondered what would happen if I looked as if I needed diamonds or a new car! Would I have caused her a nervous breakdown or a synaptic overload? Or would I have found myself bejeweled and on wheels?

I watched as the hostess was equally attentive to all in the room. We were all relieved of any responsibility, while she assumed it for all of us. It was marvelous! She gave us all the rare experience of having nothing to do but enjoy ourselves and each other's company.

There are times when it's acceptable and wonderful to have someone else take on some of our responsibilities. Yet the importance of personal responsibility can't be underestimated. I think back to the Garden of Eden, where God held each individual personally responsible for his or her part in the fall of mankind. Notice in the following excerpts from Genesis 3:14-19 how God pointed to each one involved and delivered to each his or her own consequences.

So the Lord God said to the serpent, "Because you have done this, "Cursed are you...." To the woman he said, "I will greatly increase your pains...."

To Adam he said, "Because you listened to your wife and ate from the tree ... cursed is the ground because of you; through painful toil you will eat of it all the days of your life."

GENESIS 3:14-17

Personal responsibility is the hallmark of the individual life. Not only must we accept responsibility for ourselves, we must also take great care not to infringe on the responsibilities of others. There are those of us who are somewhat like my hostess, except that we assume responsibility on a grander scale, in more areas of our lives, and for reasons other than the comfort of others. We become overly responsible as a way of feeling good about ourselves and avoiding negative repercussions. That's how it was with Fran.

Fran

Fran came to therapy with her husband, Jim. She complained about his lack of involvement in certain areas of their marriage.

"I always have to plan everything," she said. "If I don't plan it, it doesn't get done."

She was talking about their time together and the work of maintaining the marriage relationship. Jim agreed that he didn't initiate the time away or the dinners out, because Fran was so good at doing those types of things.

"But, you never do it!" she said. "You never have. It's always been me. I plan the vacations, reserve the rooms, or schedule the cruises. I don't remember signing up for this."

In actuality, Fran had, in a way, signed up to be the social coordinator of the relationship. How did she do that? Back at the beginning of the relationship, when Jim had no suggestion for such things, Fran offered hers. When she did this repeatedly, Jim began to anticipate that she'd be the one who always had the ideas, so he just let the task fall to her, and she voluntarily took it on.

What we're looking at here is a case of one person becoming over-responsible at the expense of another person who becomes underresponsible. Eventually, however, the over-responsible person usually begins to blame the underresponsible person for not contributing. Why does this happen?

Where does this weakness of being over-responsible originate?

Excessively high expectations or fear of repercussions. Some of us were raised in or have later in life spent extended periods of time in environments where expectations were excessively high. In our desire to please or to avoid repercussions we've tried to meet those expectations and, if possible, exceed them. When we move from that environment to one where expectations aren't as extreme, our behavior may then be over-responsible. Those around us may not have such high expectations, and we may develop the tendency to take over their tasks for them. As a result, they may become underresponsible.

Perfectionism. The excessive demands of those of us who are perfectionists drive us to meticulous control of everything around us. We're driven to two extremes. We either do nothing because we fear imperfection, or we overfunction, striving for perfection.

Desire for control. Our desire for control may lead us to overfunction as we try to control others.

Approval needs not being met and performance orientation. When our approval needs aren't met, we may try to earn that approval. In our quest for approval we may find it difficult to say no. This may drive our level of performance up and lead to overfunctioning.

Excessive affirmation of responsibility. If we're praised for performance at the expense of other areas of our lives, such as character development, we may invest extra energy in performance. This may lead to overfunctioning.

Traumatic or abusive backgrounds. Beyond being over-responsible in a physical sense, some of us are over-responsible when it comes to guilt. If we've been treated abusively, we may at the same time have been made to feel responsible for the abuse. We may thus take on the responsibility for actions that belongs to others.

How, then, can the weakness of over-responsibility be overcome?

▶ *Recognize that we're over-responsible.* We must recognize our own weakness in the area of over-responsibility. Do others complain that we do too much? Are we busy doing things all of the time? Are others around us doing too little while we pick up the slack for them?

▶ *Recognize and acknowledge the effects of this weakness on ourselves.* Overfunctioning will increase our levels of anxiety, agitation, and resentment.

▶ *Recognize the effects of over-responsibility on others.* Being over-responsible always costs both us and others. Those around us may become underresponsible. We need to look around and see if anyone we're close to is failing to perform because we are overperforming. Are others failing to develop their skills because we're doing too much? We need to ask ourselves how this will affect their future, and whether we're willing to be responsible for contributing to others' lack of development.

▶ *Recognize, resist, and reconsider the impulse to be over-responsible.* Quite often, those of us who are over-responsible see our behavior as sacrificial. We see it as a good thing. We must recognize that, except for unusual circumstances, being over-responsible isn't a good thing. We must look beyond ourselves and see the effects that our overresponsibility has on others. We'll most likely need to recognize how this weakness negatively affects others before we will stop doing it. We must hold our willingness to sacrifice up to the light and see that this sacrifice violates others' rights to personal development. They'll suffer because of our actions, and so will our relationships with them. In that light, our sacrifice is detrimental to others and wrong. It robs them of their opportunity for growth. When the impulse to be overresponsible strikes, we must consider the damage that can be done. This will help us to resist what is actually an impulse to harm and destroy.

If our over-responsibility is in the area of taking on others' guilt, even greater harm can be done. We'll punish ourselves for things that we didn't do. This will likely lead to low self-esteem, depression, anger, and misperception of ourselves. Furthermore, because we've taken on the guilt ourselves, those who are guilty aren't likely to face their behavior and accept responsibility for it. The possibilities for harm here are enormous.

When Fran realized that she'd contributed not only to the development of her own weakness but also to that of her husband, she had twice the reason to change. Instead of investing her emotional energy in over-responsibility and in resenting her husband, she invested that same energy in being reasonably responsible. In the process she developed strengths in the areas of compassion, being responsible, respecting the rights of others, and seeing herself and her motives accurately.

Companion Weaknesses

1√	6√	11√	16	21√	26√	31	36	41	46√
2	7√	12√	17	22√	27√	32	37	42	47√
3√	8√	13√	18√	23	28√	33	38√	43	48√
4√	9	14√	19√	24√	29	34√	39√	44	49√
5√	10	15	20	25√	30	35	40	45√	50√

It's My Way or the Highway
Weakness: Disregard of Others

On Main Street, on the way to school, was a candy store. No one, no thing, no power could keep me from stopping at that store each morning as I walked to school! Why? Only at this store could I get three pieces of pink stick chewing gum for a penny, all wrapped up nice and neat with a paper band around them, so the gum wouldn't run loose in my pockets. For a dime, I could get a six-pack of tiny wax bottles of Kool-Aid to hide in my desk for when I got thirsty. They were great because you could bite a part of the bottle off and the rest would remain sealed by the wax. No muss, no fuss. Very important to a fourth grader! Then there was the coup de gras, Pixie Sticks, all colors, all flavors, each individually wrapped and sold so you never had to buy an orange one!

Often, my little friends would encourage me to ride to school with them, but that was a no go. Either they'd have to walk with me or I'd go it alone. Deep snowdrifts wouldn't stop me from walking to school. If offered a ride, I would decline. While other tykes of lesser stock chickened out and succumbed to the bus, I held firm. My way was the only way to get to school, and I yielded to no one on the matter!

There are times when we should not compromise, when we should instead hold fast, no matter the consequence. Yet, more often than not, it is a better thing to give up ground than to lose the people around us. Gary learned this lesson the hard way.

Gary

Gary was a visionary. Like most visionaries, Gary saw the big picture. He knew where he wanted to take his business. He knew the heights it could reach. The problem, according to Gary, was with those under him who were negative and complainers. He saw them as being disloyal to the vision and to him.

Gary's staff brought to his attention many positive accounts of the business, but they also tried to alert him to potential and real issues as well. He was open to hearing the good things, but not the bad ones. He didn't want to hear about the bad things because he didn't want to consider problems that could affect his vision. He simply insisted that his staff deal with these problems and make them go away.

To the general population, Gary seemed to be strong, successful, and confident, a leader among leaders. However, to his staff he had become a tyrant. Their attempts to communicate with him were often met with hostility and recriminations. He had hired them to handle those things with which he didn't want to deal. His only agenda was to make the vision real. While this was the same vision shared by his staff, they had to deal with the problematic details.

I was brought into the company to advise Gary and his staff as to how to handle this situation. After listening to Gary and his staff, it seemed clear to me that to Gary, the vision wasn't more important than his staff. It was, however, more important than their complaints. His staff wasn't able to make this distinction and saw his frustrations as personal assaults against them. This wasn't surprising, since Gary's method of communication clearly targeted the individual.

The staff saw Gary's behavior as harmful and as a type of disregard for them. Yet, the salaries paid to the staff clearly demonstrated Gary's regard for their worth. This left them with a confusing sense of both approval and disapproval. They often felt guilty if they became angry with Gary for his behavior.

The solution to the problem required Gary and his staff to consider each other's perspectives. As Gary listened to his staff he tended to lump all of their complaints into one category when, in fact, there were several different types of complaints. Some were items that required his attention. Others were reactions to his not listening to the first complaint. If Gary had taken care of the initial complaints, there would've been no follow-up complaints.

The staff failed to see that as the public head of the company, Gary wanted to be careful not to adapt to any negative attitude. He wanted to be insulated from that. Yet, he had a dual role. He had to represent the company and run it at the same time. The representation required that he be positive and upbeat. The other required that he deal with the negative information.

Essentially, what was happening was that these two roles hadn't been made clear to the staff, and they therefore had not been equipped with communication methods that would make the information palatable to Gary. For this reason, Gary had no way of hearing negative information without it placing him under extraordinary stress, at which point he would act out, inappropriately and harmfully.

What's the origin of this weakness of disregard for others?

Stress. Gary mistreated his staff under the stress of their complaints. In order to remedy this situation, he had to first admit and address his own harmful behavior, for which he was fully responsible. Then, he had to equip his staff with the tools they needed to provide what he expected of them.

Excessive self-sufficiency. Those who say "It's my way or the highway" have issues with control, self-centeredness, and a disregard for others. Yet, there's another player in the mix. Those who say such things value having their way more than they value the presence of others. They're self-sufficient to an unhealthy degree and are willing to dispense with others rather than to reach a healthy compromise.

Privileged expectation. Some of us were raised with an excessive amount of praise or privilege. We're accustomed to being deferred to, and may not even realize the extent of our disregard for others.

Insecurity and control. Some of us are unsure of ourselves. Because of this, we demand our way. Our arrogance and demands are fronts for our lack of self-assurance. Many of us don't feel secure unless we have control. We value control more than we do people.

How do we overcome the weakness of disregard for others?

▸ *Listen.* We must welcome criticism rather than despising it. If there's any truth in it, it'll give us an indication of what needs improvement in our lives. Criticism is often the pathway to growth and development. We must learn to treat it as just that.

▸ *Appreciate.* We must learn to appreciate people for who they are, not just for what they bring to us. To do otherwise is dehumanizing. The people in our lives are more important than what they can do for us.

▸ *Review and restore.* At every indicator that we're showing disregard for others, we need to stop in our tracks and review our core values. We need to question if they've been compromised. If we say we care about people yet we treat them with disregard, then that value has been compromised. When this happens we need to review our core values and restore them to the place of power they should hold in our lives. The risk here is a compromise of character, which we can't afford.

Gary and the members of his staff had to do these very things. The effort they invested here was effort extracted from the weakness of disregard for others and from additional weaknesses. Among the strengths developed by Gary and his staff members were: compassion, honesty, openness, respect, healthy communication, forgiveness, and integrity.

Companion Weaknesses

1	6√	11√	16	21√	26	31	36	41√	46√
2	7√	12	17√	22	27	32√	37√	42√	47√
3√	8√	13√	18√	23	28√	33	38√	43√	48√
4	9	14	19√	24	29	34	39	44	49√
5√	10√	15	20	25√	30	35	40	45√	50√

You Just Don't Listen!
Weakness: The Tendency to Demand Agreement

Imagine some mathematician insisting to Albert Einstein that $e = mc^3$! All the while Einstein knows that $e = mc^2$. Imagine that over and over again this mathematician insists to Einstein, each time more forcefully, that $e = mc^3$. Then he insists that Einstein is just not listening, that he just doesn't understand. He doesn't get it!

Would we agree that Einstein wasn't listening or that he didn't understand? After all, it was Einstein who determined that, in fact, $e = mc^2$. Certainly he would listen, understand, and get it. Yet he would not agree with the erring mathematician. This is similar to what happens quite often in my office. Sam is a good example.

Sam

"The only way to deal with your brother is to shut him out!" Sam said.

"I can't do that, Sam. He's my brother!" said Barbara, his wife.

"You just don't get it, Barb!" he said. "He's never going to do what we want him to do. He's never going to pay us what he owes us. He's never going to put things back where he got them. He's never going to stop interrupting me."

"I know all that!" Barbara said. "You've said it a thousand times. I don't need to hear it again! I just don't want to kick him out on the street."

"You're not listening to me, Barb!" Sam insisted. "I'm telling you he's never going to change. He's never going to do what we want him to do!"

I intervened by asking Sam what he was after. He said that all he wanted was for Barbara to listen to him and understand what he was saying. I then asked Barbara to repeat what Sam had said and explain what she thought he meant. She was accurate.

"It looks like Barbara has heard you and understood you, Sam," I said. "So, what else are you looking for?"

"Well, she doesn't understand or she'd kick her brother out!" he replied.

"So, what you're looking for is for her to agree with you?" I asked.

"No," he said. "I just want her to see what's going on."

I had Barbara repeat back to Sam what she thought was going on, and once again she was accurate. It took several more rounds of this clarification before Sam was able to see what he was doing.

Sam was under the mistaken impression that Barbara didn't understand him or didn't listen to him. That was the repeated theme in all that he said. Yet that's not what was happening. Barbara heard and understood him. She just didn't agree with him. Sam was pressing Barbara to get her to agree with him. However, Sam didn't know that this was what he was doing. He genuinely thought that he was just trying to get her to listen.

Once the real issue was clarified, we were able to have some reasonable discussions of their differences of opinion. And yes, the brother did move out.

What's the origin of this weakness of demanding agreement?

Thinking in absolutes. When someone thinks predominantly in terms of right and wrong, or in terms of black and white, there's a tendency to demand agreement. In these situations, only one person can be right, and that means the other person must be wrong. Since no one wants to be wrong, the tendency will be to fight to be right, to demand agreement.

Previous environments of absolutes. Some of us have experienced situations where one person held the power to be right, and only that person's opinion was allowed. If there's no middle ground and we must be either right or wrong, we will fight to be right. No one wants to be wrong. This was the case with Sam's childhood environment.

Insecurity and fear. When we're insecure, we may demand agreement in order to avoid the pain of being wrong, being seen as wrong, or being rejected. This demand for agreement can be particularly tenacious, painful, and confusing. This is because the person who's demanding agreement and causing the difficulty is at the same time desperate for approval.

Pride. We may demand agreement because we consider our opinion to be the only one worth considering.

Security investment. Some of us have lived in threatening environments where our awareness of potential dangers in the environment may have been what kept us safe. We may have begun to have a security investment in having information and being right about it. If this is the case, any challenge to our being right will be a threat to our sense of security. This will trigger our anger and self-defense.

So, how can we overcome the weakness of demanding agreement?

▶ *Recognize and admit.* We need to listen to ourselves. Are we pushing our point to the extent that, rather than an opinion, it becomes a demand for agreement?

▶ *Consider the listener.* Is the person with whom we are arguing someone who is not able to understand us, or does this person simply not agree? If we're unsure as to whether someone has heard us, we can ask him or her to repeat what we've said. If the person gets the basics correct, the problem isn't that he or she doesn't understand. It's that he or she doesn't agree.

▶ *Respect.* We must respect the rights of others to disagree.

▶ *Resist.* If we've made our point once and then restated it, we must resist the urge to say it again. Beyond that point we become demanding.

Once Sam was able to see what he was doing, things changed. At that point he was able to see that his wife really did listen and understand. He also saw that he was misrepresenting her, and stopped doing this. In addition, he had to learn how to handle disagreement and to respect others' opinions. Rerouting his emotional and intellectual energies away from his weakness of demanding agreement, Sam could invest them elsewhere. He developed strengths related to respecting others, listening, understanding himself and others, patience, and healthy debate.

Companion Weaknesses

1√	6√	11√	16√	21√	26√	31√	36	41√	46√
2	7	12√	17√	22	27√	32√	37	42√	47√
3√	8√	13√	18√	23	28√	33√	38√	43√	48√
4√	9	14√	19√	24√	29	34√	39√	44√	49√
5√	10	15√	20	25	30√	35	40√	45√	50√

SIX

Extremes and Excesses of Thought and Behavior

In my younger years, I was taken for a visit to the local dentist. I don't know if I'd been to a dentist prior to that, but I doubt it. If I had, I think there would've been a wanted poster in the waiting room just in case I showed up again.

I sat there, in the dentist chair, with drills all around me, a suction tube hanging out of my mouth, and someone telling me to rinse and spit. This didn't seem to me to be a safe place for a child, which is what I was.

I was doing my best to comply with the dentist's demands when, while he had his hand in my mouth, he touched a very sensitive nerve and, yes, I bit him. Well, he'd told me to let him know if anything hurt. So I did! After all, I couldn't have said to him, "I'm sorry, Mr. Dentist. We'll need to stop for just a few moments while I recuperate from the excruciating pain you've just caused me by tapping against a tooth I already told you was hurting!"

I recall walking out of the dentist's office, holding hands with my mother, who was muttering something like, "I'm never taking you to the dentist again!" It seems that my mother thought my method of communicating my pain to the dentist was somewhat extreme and perhaps excessive. Yet, my perspective was different.

I thought my tiny bite was a very clear, concise, and efficient means of communication. I saw it as a reasonable response to the dentist's ill-fated excursion into the deeper recesses of my mouth. To me, what seemed extreme to both my mother and the dentist wasn't extreme at all. I thought that within the context of the situation, it was actually understandable.

Everything I Do Is Wrong
Weakness: The Tendency to Be Extreme in Thinking

Apparently there are certain unspoken requirements for being a teenager. First, a teen must be able to live as close to the definition of psychosis as possible without truly being psychotic. Second, a teen must have a well-developed ability to focus on any possible technicality that could be to his or her advantage and not to yours. Finally, a teen must think and speak exclusively and fluently in extremes.

Teenagers often live in the land of fantastic, horrible, terrible, great, and incredible. Things don't seem to happen, or not happen, just once. It's every time, always, or never. There's no adjustment to life, just the end of the world. Words like "often" or "occasionally" are strictly prohibited!

This type of extreme thinking and extreme communication is a part of what drives teenage behavior to such roller-coaster highs and lows. It's evidence that teenagers are learning about their own emotional extremities. This can be a healthy thing for a teenager if it's a transient experience. Yet, continuing to live in extremes isn't healthy. Anna's story is a good example.

Anna

"I can't handle this anymore," Anna said. "Everything I do is wrong! I can't get anything right! My husband thinks I'm the worst parent in the world. The kids hate me. I can't take this anymore."

Every one of Anna's sentences contained extreme words or thoughts. Aside from the problems she was actually experiencing, she was driving her feelings higher with the words she was using. Anna's use of extreme thoughts and their accompanying words contributed to her depression.

When we think extreme thoughts or use extreme words, our emotions will adjust to meet the extremity of the word or thought. If I say things are horrible, I'll likely experience heightened emotions that'll try to match the extremity of that word. The more extreme the words we use, the more extreme the feelings they produce.

These extreme thoughts can provide us with a distorted sense of reality. We may call something horrible when it's actually just uncomfortable. We may think the end of the world has come when actually only an adjustment is needed. We may think of something as impossible when it's just difficult. When we start to live in response to these distortions, we begin to live in a distorted reality. Others are drawn into that distorted reality when they react to us.

The underlying culprit in all of this is the extreme thinking.

Where does the weakness of extreme thinking originate?

Modeling. We learn what's modeled to us, whether by family, peers, or culture. If those around us speak or live in extremes, that'll be our tendency as well. If we're in relationships with others who exhibit extreme thinking, we may begin to think in extremes as well.

Insecurity. Those of us who are insecure tend to read what we're afraid of into situations. We tend to think in terms of worst-case scenarios. This leads to extreme thinking.

Crisis Orientation. If we've lived in tumultuous environments we may be conditioned to think in terms of crisis or potential crisis. Crisis thoughts are extreme. "Something horrible is going to happen if I don't...." Anna was raised in a chaotic family and developed a crisis orientation in her thinking and behavior.

Perfectionism. Perfectionism is extreme at its core. Everything has to be perfect. Perfectionists think in extremes.

How do we overcome the weakness of extreme thinking?

▶ *Recognize.* We need to recognize extreme thoughts. They can be all encompassing, absolutes, superlatives, or representative of extreme concepts or states. Some examples are such terms as *all, every, none, never, hopeless, helpless, awful,* and *terrible.*

▸ *Conform.* We need to conform our thoughts and words to the current reality: That terrified me as a child. Should it terrify me now as an adult? Is this a horrible experience or just an uncomfortable experience? Do I hate this or just not like it?

▸ *Develop and use continuum thinking.* We must develop a vocabulary of middle ground. Feeling nothing and feeling terror are extremes, and they're not the only options. Some examples of more moderate feelings include: uncomfortable, uneasy, frightened, troubled, bothered, and unpleasant.

Anna began to feel relief from her stress as soon as she began to correct her internal dialogue. She withdrew emotional and intellectual energy from her weakness of extreme thinking and invested it instead in learning to eliminate extreme thoughts. In doing so, Anna developed strengths in the areas of truth, emotional stability, and clear thinking.

Companion Weaknesses

1√	6√	11√	16√	21√	26	31	36	41√	46√
2	7	12√	17√	22	27√	32√	37	42	47√
3√	8√	13√	18√	23√	28√	33√	38√	43√	48√
4√	9√	14√	19	24	29√	34√	39√	44√	49√
5√	10	15	20	25√	30√	35√	40√	45√	50√

I Tend to Be Destructive
Weakness: The Tendency to Be Extreme in Behavior

I remember the beautiful blue sky gently peeking through the tall trees as I glided on my cross-country skis through the glistening snow. All I could hear was the sound of pristine snow being swept aside by my skis. There were no sounds of people, phones, automobiles, or airplanes. No gasoline fumes or smog, only the scent of the trees in the crisp Rocky Mountain air. If I held still, the only thing I could hear was the sound of my own breathing. With the exception of occasional wildlife, I was utterly alone, miles into the mountainous terrain. The serenity brought me to tears. How could someone experience this, see this, and not know there's a loving God?

This was an extreme experience. It's not recommended to trek out alone into the winter Rocky Mountain wilderness. It can be unsafe. This extreme adventure was truly awe-inspiring. Yet, I could've ended up as some bear's lunch, a renegade hunter's trophy, or an adult-size popsicle!

There are times for extremes. We give our all for competitive events or special occasions. We dash out of the way of an oncoming car. However, extremes are often unhealthy and sometimes downright dangerous. Bill's story is a good example of extreme behavior.

Bill

Bill's wife found the cocaine in his jacket pocket. She'd suspected that he was using again. He'd been working exceedingly late, unable to sleep, and taking long walks at night, and his alcohol consumption had increased. Then he was gone for two days without explanation. He came to my office at the wrong end of an ultimatum. He either had to quit or leave.

This was Bill's third relapse, and there were no drug or alcohol programs in town that he hadn't tried. He was coming to me as a last resort. I didn't hold any guarantees, either. Bill seemed determined to destroy his life. I needed to know why. Why was he engaging in extreme, high-risk behaviors?

Bill's successful business had just gone public. At the very pinnacle of success he left the office, went to a sleazy hotel, closed the curtains, and consumed cocaine all night long. He wasn't celebrating. He was medicating. He was trying to cover his feelings of anxiety and fear and confirm his feelings of low self-worth. That's one of the attractive attributes of drug abuse. It does many things at the same time. It's efficient, an equal-opportunity destroyer, one-stop shopping. By the time you've figured out why you're doing drugs, the reason has changed. Now you're doing it for the drugs themselves. This was Bill's predicament.

Why do some people tend to be so extreme in their behaviors that they become destructive? What is the origin of this weakness of unhealthy extreme behaviors?

Adjusting to past levels of anxiety. When we've experienced a chronically tension-filled or volatile environment we may seek extreme, high-adrenaline behaviors to make us feel alive. We need to have an experience that rises higher than our internal level of anxiety.

Compensating for depression. In the face of a deep, dark depression, we may engage in extreme or dangerous behaviors. We do this in order to feel something other than depression.

Self-punishment and self-validation. If we've come from abusive backgrounds we may engage in extreme and dangerous behaviors in order to force the world to punish us so that we can prove to ourselves that we're as bad as we've been led to believe we are.

Quieting feelings. When guilt or anxiety rise up in us, we may seek to quiet it with something more powerful, something that conceals or cloaks our feelings of guilt or anxiety.

Forcing correction. We may engage in extreme or dangerous behaviors in order to dare fate and try to force its hand. We may have begun to feel that we don't care about ourselves. We may dare the rest of the world to show us that it cares, even if this is done with a negative or punishing response.

Altering mood. We may engage in extreme behaviors to eliminate feelings of boredom, emptiness, sadness, or grief.

Perfectionism. We may think that everything has to be perfect and drive ourselves to extreme behaviors in order to accomplish this.

Self-hate. We may hate ourselves and seek our own destruction. We may hate someone else and seek to punish him or her with our destructive behaviors.

Altering image. We may feel the pressure of maintaining a good image and want to change it from good to bad.

Extreme beliefs. We may hold to extreme beliefs that lead to extreme behavior.

So, how do we overcome the weakness of extreme behavior?

▸ *Acknowledge our weakness.* We need to acknowledge that we're investing a great deal of energy in a destructive weakness that could be invested instead in the greatness that belongs to us.

▸ *Evaluate our motives.* When it comes to extremes, the difference between greatness and tragedy is whether or not the motives and methods are meant for good. The rudiments of greatness are found in extreme behaviors. There we find the ability, determination, and courage to take risks.

▸ *Determine our focus.* We need to determine who we want to be and let that determination drive how we choose to behave.

▸ *Seek accountability.* We need to share our vision of who we want to be with someone who'll hold us accountable for our actions.

Bill saw himself using cocaine. That picture, that definition of himself, drove his behavior. When he withdrew cocaine from the picture and saw himself as a successful husband and businessman, his desire for cocaine lessened. Bill determined that any extremes in which he would be involved would have to be motivated by the intention and desire to do what was good and right. He rerouted all of his efforts toward this goal and developed strengths related to honesty, dependability, loyalty, and spiritual growth.

Companion Weaknesses

1√	6	11	16√	21√	26√	31	36	41√	46√
2√	7√	12√	17	22	27	32√	37	42	47√
3√	8√	13√	18	23	28√	33√	38√	43√	48√
4√	9√	14√	19√	24√	29√	34√	39√	44	49√
5√	10	15√	20√	25	30√	35√	40√	45√	50√

I Have No Middle Ground
Weakness: The Tendency to Be Emotionally Reactive

Perfectionists are some of the most vulnerable people on earth. They're among the easiest to drive insane. Would you like to know how? Here are a few suggestions.

You know that hall closet that no one ever looks into or uses? When your perfectionist asks you to paint it Navajo White, paint it Antique White instead. Go ahead and nail the door shut and I promise you the perfectionist will still know what you've done.

Here's another one. When your perfectionist tells you to do something, try to negotiate with him or her. Ask if you can clean the garage on Friday at three o'clock instead of on Saturday at eight o'clock. A few seconds later, change your mind and ask if you can do it on Saturday at noon instead of on Saturday at eight o'clock. Then just stand back and wait for the nervous tic to start.

Here's one more. When you ask your perfectionist to do something for you, give him or her options and let him or her decide. Tell this person you would appreciate his or her help. Your perfectionist may take the car to the garage or call the guy about the termites and schedule him to come out. Then ask the perfectionist which one he or she would rather do. The likely response will be, "I don't care. Just pick one!" If you do this to a perfectionist three times in the same day, he or she will short-circuit. You'll be able to smell the burnt wires and can see the steam coming out of his or her ears.

Why does this happen? It's because perfectionists are emotionally reactive and they have no middle ground. It's all or nothing with them. If you propose otherwise, their circuits overload. And they're not the only ones who short-circuit. Brad is a good example.

Brad's Wife

Brad told me about a recent encounter with his wife. He'd come home from work fifteen minutes late. When he arrived, his wife met him at the door, screaming at him.

"Where have you been? Why didn't you call? Were you with someone?" She kept at him.

Brad became angry and told her to back off, but she demanded an answer. He yelled back that he hadn't done anything wrong.

She threatened, "Don't you ever do this to me again!"

Brad threw his hands in the air and said, "All right! Now get off my back!" and walked away.

This is a perfect example of emotional reactivity. Brad's wife's reaction to his being fifteen minutes late was an extreme overreaction. It was much greater than the circumstance warranted.

Emotional reactivity occurs when someone has an emotional reaction to a situation that's larger than the situation warrants. That reaction alone is a problem, but it also generates other problems. It's like a nuclear reaction. One atomic particle hits another, which hits another, and the explosive reactions continue and multiply, speeding up until there's a catastrophic explosion.

Where does the weakness of emotional reactivity originate?

Past experiences. People become emotionally reactive when their intense emotional investment in an area is accessed through some emotional pipeline. Brad's wife had been married previously to someone who was unfaithful. She still suffered pain from that past infidelity. It was like living inside of a bruise. The bruise that had been caused by her past experience hadn't healed completely. When that bruise was touched, the pain was greater than it would normally have been. Her reaction was more about her past than about Brad.

The need to control. Those of us who are controlling are intent on accomplishing our agendas. We tend to be emotionally reactive if something is out of our control.

Emotional investment. An intense emotional investment in certain ideologies or ways of believing can lead to emotional reactivity. Perfectionists tend to be emotionally reactive because they believe that they or others should do things a certain way. Religious beliefs or extreme patriotism may also lead to emotionally reactive responses.

How can the weakness of emotional reactivity be overcome?

▶ *Identify the tendency to be emotionally reactive.* We must question every emotional reaction.

▶ *Stop and question.* At the point of the extreme emotional reaction, we need to stop and question, "Is this reaction greater than the current circumstance warrants?" If so, we need to ask, "Why is this so important to me? Is there something in my past that makes me especially sensitive to this issue?" If we determine that there's a connection between the current circumstance and a past issue, we need to ask ourselves whether we are letting the past influence the current situation. If the answer is yes, we need to be sure that the degree of influence this past issue is having on the current circumstance is appropriate.

For instance, if, as in the case with Brad's wife, a past male figure has been unfaithful, it makes sense for us to be sensitive to the issue. Yet, if the current man in our life has never been unfaithful, we shouldn't read into his behaviors more than is there.

▶ *Relegate.* If we can separate yesterday's experience from today's, yesterday's issues are more likely to take their places in the past, where they belong.

▶ *Seek truth and middle ground.* We need to look for truth and middle ground. Just because one man has been unfaithful doesn't mean that every man or that a particular other man will be unfaithful. Some may be. Some may not.

Brad understood that his wife was struggling with a weakness of emotional reactivity. He helped her to understand what was happening, and over time they worked together to conquer her weakness. She took the energy previously invested in her weakness and invested it instead in developing strength in the area of trust.

Companion Weaknesses

1√	6√	11√	16√	21√	26√	31√	36	41√	46√
2√	7	12√	17√	22	27√	32√	37	42√	47√
3√	8√	13√	18√	23	28	33√	38√	43	48√
4√	9√	14√	19√	24√	29√	34√	39√	44	49√
5√	10	15√	20	25√	30√	35√	40√	45√	50√

We're Either Emotionally Dominated or Too Cognitive
Weakness: Lack of Integration

I knew a guy once who spoke science. Every time I'd start a conversation with him it'd take only a few moments before he'd interrupt with some sort of question or comment on the earth's volcanic core or astrophysics. Those of us who were there would collectively roll our eyes and sigh in utter exasperation.

Kyle was hopeless. We all knew it. At one point we considered taking up a collection to get Kyle a brain transplant, but it was too expensive. We just never could get him to come in for a landing. He lived in the ozone layer, as far as we could tell, all by himself. Even when he was with us, he really wasn't. I admit that Kyle was a bit extreme, but there are many others who struggle in similar ways. Tim is a good example.

Tim

Tim related mostly to concepts or thoughts. He understood very little about feelings, relating only to anger and frustration. He didn't really emotionally connect with anyone. Tim could talk to you splendidly about politics, religion, and travel, almost anything you wanted to talk about. Yet, ask Tim what he was feeling and he could answer only with what he thought.

"How do you feel when you hear your wife say that you aren't meeting her emotional needs?" I asked Tim.

"I think she wants me to do something I'm obviously not doing," Tim responded.

"How do you think you would feel if she wasn't meeting your needs?" I asked, checking his ability to empathize emotionally.

"I think I'd say something about it, just like she's doing," Tim said.

Tim's wife, Mary Dean, was taking all of this in from the other end of the couch. Out of the corner of my eye I could see her relax into sad tears as she recognized that someone besides herself saw what the problem was. It's very hard on people when they're inside a marriage where others can clearly see their pain, yet no one else can see or understand their confusion. I suppose there's no lonelier place than a marriage at times like that.

Like Tim, we all face certain problems if our means of relating to others is limited to only what we think. Emotional connection, essential to healthy relationship, requires us to be able to identify and talk about our feelings. Furthermore, it requires us to be able to listen to the feelings of others and relate to them.

The only complaint that Tim's wife had was that he wasn't there emotionally. Because of this, neither one's emotional needs were being met. Mary Dean felt significant guilt, in that Tim provided well in every other way but this one. She feared that her complaining would be an indication that she was ungrateful, which she wasn't. The fact was that all other needs could be met, yet without emotional connection they felt painfully unfinished, at times agonizingly empty. Few things are more difficult or painful than standing beside the love of your life and yet not being able to reach him or her.

I was careful to quickly remind both Tim and Mary Dean that Tim was, in fact, able to feel. We knew that because he could become frustrated or angry. The problem was that he didn't know how to access other feelings.

Later we will see how Tim's background played into his being overly dominated by his cognitive abilities at the expense of his feelings. Yet there is another side to the thought versus emotion coin. Deanne is an example of someone who was dominated by her emotions at the expense of her thoughts.

Deanne

Deanne was having extreme problems in her relationships with friends. She seemed to be overwhelmed by their emotional problems. It was as if their problems were hers. There seemed to be no separation between her feelings and theirs.

"I can't be around Sue," Deanne said. "It's too painful. She's dealing with so much right now, and it's just too painful."

"Painful for whom?" I asked.

"For her, of course, and it's painful for me, too," she responded. "Her husband, David, is having an affair and now the kids have found out. It's horrible. She calls and I just cringe when I hear the pain in her voice."

"How are you helping her?" I asked.

"I try to give her support. I tell her how to talk to the kids. I listen to her when she needs me to. I also calm her down by telling her that this is a crisis and that she needs to remember that things are worse in a crisis and not to act just on her feelings. I tell her that David does love her and that he doesn't want to leave her. That calms her to some degree," she explained.

"It sounds like you are a big help to her right now," I commented.

"Yes, but the pain is enormous," she said, "and it's all I can do to be there for her. It's getting to be more than I can handle."

"You're so good at helping her. How do you help yourself?" I asked. "What do you say to yourself that'll bring you comfort and support during this time?"

"I don't know," she said. "I just tell myself to be strong because she needs me right now."

If we look closely, we can see that Deanne helped her friend Sue separate her feelings from her thoughts. She knew instinctively to direct Sue to thoughts that would calm her. Yet Deanne didn't seem to be able to do that for herself. When it came to helping herself, Deanne subscribed only to thoughts that drove her emotions to a greater intensity.

Failing to challenge the thoughts behind our emotions, in any area of our lives, leaves us vulnerable in that area to immaturity. Growing up requires a gradual leaning toward reason consistent with truth as the governing force in our lives. Emotional reasoning is fueled by extremes and inaccuracies in thinking. The result is often emotional reactivity and, as with Deanne, a feeling of being overwhelmed.

Why was it that Deanne could help Sue with her thoughts and emotions but couldn't help herself? Why was it that Tim, in the previous example, could experience anger but not other emotions? Why was he so dominated by his thoughts at the expense of his feelings?

What's the origin of the weaknesses of extremes of emotional or cognitive domination?

Modeling. We may learn, as Tim did, to avoid talking about feelings. Tim was raised in a non-emotive environment, where his parents didn't talk about feelings and where love was shown by actions, not stated out loud. In addition, Tim was never taught how to relate to or express emotions.

On the other hand, if we repeatedly see a parent or another important person in our lives demonstrate emotional dominance, we may be impacted by that modeling. It may become our learned behavior.

Traumatic environment. Some of us have lived in traumatic environments where we've not been allowed to express our feelings. In those environments we may have felt unsafe or worried that our feelings might overwhelm us, and so we may have shut down our feelings and banished them from our awareness. Once this happens, we become progressively removed from our feelings and more reliant upon our cognitive capabilities. One becomes overdeveloped at the expense of the other.

The same factors may be at work with emotional domination. Deanne's upbringing was without much in the way of conflict. However, she later married someone who verbally and emotionally abused her. There was so much conflict in the marriage that Deanne began to anticipate the worst. She began to think in extremes, driven by fear, until those extreme thoughts became automatic. At some point, her thoughts became fused to her emotions and it became difficult to tell them apart. Eventually the distinction was disregarded and

Deanne began to live solely according to her feelings.

How do we overcome the weakness of cognitive domination?

▶ *Learn to identify and name feelings.* Emotional connection requires a feeling vocabulary. We need to learn words that express emotions, and then practice using them.

▶ *Learn to identify with others' feelings.* We need to listen to others as they talk about feelings and ask them more about their experience. We need to question ourselves whether we've ever felt that way about anything. This will us help relate emotionally to others.

In order to overcome the weakness of emotional domination, we must:

▶ *Identify feelings and challenge the thoughts behind them.* Our feelings are driven by our thoughts. If our thoughts are in error, then our emotions will be consistent with that error. Therefore, we must not automatically trust our feelings. We must first determine what thought is behind the feeling.

▶ *Conform thinking to current truth.* Once we've identified our feelings and discovered the thoughts behind each of them, we need to conform those thoughts to the current reality.

Tim and Deanne addressed their respective weaknesses, and in time both developed strengths in integrating thoughts and feelings, self-evaluation, telling the whole truth, and living according to that truth.

SIX: EXTREMES AND EXCESSES / 149

Companion Weaknesses (Cognitive Domination)

1	6	1N	16	2N	26	31	36	4N	46√
2	7N	12	17	22N	27	32N	37	42N	47N
3	8	13	18	23√	28	33	38	43√	48
4	9	14	19	24	29	34	39	44	49√
5	10N	15	20	25	30N	35	40	45√	50N

Companion Weaknesses (Emotional Domination)

1N	6√	1N	16√	2N	26√	3N	36√	4N	46√
2N	7	12N	17N	22	27N	32N	37	42	47N
3N	8√	13N	18	23	28√	33N	38√	43	48√
4N	9N	14N	19	24N	29	34N	39N	44	49N
5√	10	15	20N	25√	30N	35√	40N	45√	50N

We're Either Loners or Never Alone
Weakness: The Tendencies to Be Solo or Dependent

I could live a good deal of the time in a cave. Of course, it would have to have all of the usual amenities: a feeding tube attached to my favorite restaurant, my hairdresser on speed dial, cable TV even though I watch only a few stations, church on cable, and a car in the garage, because I know I'd last only so long without contact with others. Yet some people don't seem to need others. Simon was a good example.

Simon
"He has no friends," Charlotte said of her husband. "When my friends and their husbands come over, Simon goes into the computer room and disappears for hours."

"I don't like sitting around talking about nothing," Simon said. "It's just not me."

Simon admitted that he tended to go off on his own whenever the opportunity arose. It wasn't that he didn't have anything interesting to say. He was quite intelligent and interesting. He just tended to feel anxious around others. He felt genuinely comfortable only around his wife and kids.

Some of us, like Simon, are uncomfortable in social situations. We lack interest in casual conversation and often find it so frustrating that we avoid it. Since much of social life is centered on such conversation, we pull back and become isolated. We tend to become loners.

Simon represents one side of this extreme coin, the tendency to isolate and become a loner. On the other side of the coin is Kristen, who is an example of someone tending toward dependence.

Kristen

Mindy and Kristen, sisters, came to the office together to resolve frustrations that had developed within their relationship since Kristen's divorce.

Mindy was married with two boys. Kristen had no children. Recently, Paul, Mindy's husband, had begun to complain about the amount of time Mindy was spending away from home. A part of that time was spent with Kristen and the rest of the time Mindy spent volunteering at a shelter for abused women.

"I get angry when I call as I've been asked to call and Mindy acts cold and angry," Kristen began to explain. "I suggest we get together and we do, but Mindy is so cranky. I ask her what's wrong and she says that nothing is wrong. I'm tired of being treated this way. I thought we were friends!"

I asked Mindy if what Kristen had said was true, and she said that it was.

"Why do you get angry when Kristen calls, and why are you cranky when you get together?" I asked.

"I don't know. I guess I just feel pressured," Mindy said.

"Pressured by whom?" Kristen asked.

"I don't know," Mindy said. "I don't know if it's you or Paul or the kids. I don't know."

"Do you get angry at Paul or the kids over this issue?" I asked.

"I don't think so," Mindy replied.

"So, it's about Kristen then?" I asked. "What is it that makes you feel that Kristen is putting pressure on you?"

Kristen spoke up, saying, "I told you that you could tell me you were busy or that you had other things to do."

Mindy's silence indicated her confusion.

"Could it be that the pressure is coming from within you?" I asked Mindy.

That question led us into a labyrinth of discussion and at last an understanding of what was actually going on. In reality, Mindy wanted to spend time with Kristen but felt that it was taking too much time from home. She was angry with herself for not pulling back from their relationship, and that anger was spilling over onto Kristen.

On the other hand, Kristen was someone who didn't really want to be alone. She knew she was putting pressure on Mindy but she wasn't taking any responsibility for it. She didn't have to, because Mindy was, as usual, taking responsibility for everything. Kristen's desperation to avoid being alone and Mindy's caretaking tendencies played into one another. The result was that neither one of them was being completely honest.

Mindy didn't want to place any responsibility on Kristen, because she'd then have reason to be angry with Kristen and in expressing her anger might risk losing Kristen. Mindy knew that with Kristen it was all or nothing. She was consumed in their relationship, and that made Mindy feel important. Yet there was also a constant threat that if the relationship wasn't all, it would be nothing at all. That, in itself, bound the relationship more tightly. The relationship between Mindy and Kristen thus became a dependent one, and eventually became hostile.

Where do the weaknesses of isolation and dependency originate?

Insecurity or fear. Some of us may not feel secure with who we are, or we may be afraid of being alone. The first will encourage isolation and the second will encourage dependency.

Skills deficits. If we've lived in a traumatic environment, as both Kristen and Simon had, we may have had to focus on survival. Existing in a state of survival tends out of necessity to encourage a preoccupation with self. That internal preoccupation, coupled with concentration on survival, exists at the expense of learning other things.

Lack of friends. Being self-focused inhibits our ability to make friends. For one thing, we tend to stay to ourselves. Furthermore, if we were raised in a home where we were hesitant to bring our friends home, we may also have failed to learn to socialize comfortably. Socializing to us may be a chore and extremely uncomfortable.

Limited perspective. Pulling inside of ourselves also limits our perspective in general. We may have the tendency to think that we're the only ones who feel as we do. What we're experiencing, only we're experiencing. This produces in us a tendency to be intense. Yet, we should look at our families and ask these questions: Am I the only one who is isolated? Am I the only one in this family having problems? If we don't look beyond ourselves we won't see the entire context of our difficulty. That will reinforce our sense of isolation.

We have two extremes, though. We may be loners, but we may also become dependent. Quite often we vacillate back and forth between the two conditions. When we do enter a relationship, we need control, so we're good with just one friend because we have a good deal of control in that situation. We're not good in groups. We're also capable of instant depth, and we're intense; both characteristics help to create deep relationships quickly. All of this sets us up for quickly becoming dependent upon one person.

Our social skills may be underdeveloped for a number of possible reasons, including a lack of an adequate model of positive social behavior and no experience with positive social situations. This is a part of what keeps us isolated. The skills we do have, such as the ability to go to instant depth, encourage both isolation and dependency.

So, how do we overcome the weaknesses of isolation and dependency?

▶ *Take responsibility for ourselves and our development.* If we have skills deficits, we must correct them. If we suffer from insecurity or fear, we need to address it and move beyond it.

Simon and Kristen both took on the hard task of changing their relationship styles.

Kristen and Mindy couldn't manage a healthy friendship, so their friendship lessened. As painful as this was, however, they took comfort in knowing they did the right thing for each other. They moved on and developed other relationships. Interestingly enough, on the way to becoming healthy, they each went through a relationship similar to the one they'd shared. This helped them both to take responsibility for the problems in their relationship, since it demonstrated that obviously they both had issues. Both developed strengths in the areas of personal responsibility and accountability.

Simon took some chances and faced his discomfort. He practiced socializing and talking about feelings. He laughs a bit at it all now. It wasn't as hard as he thought it would be. He developed strengths in developing relationships and taking responsibility for himself.

Companion Weaknesses (Loner)

1√	6√	11√	16√	21√	26√	31	36	41√	46√
2√	7√	12√	17√	22√	27√	32√	37	42√	47√
3√	8√	13√	18√	23	28√	33√	38√	43√	48√
4√	9	14√	19√	24√	29√	34√	39√	44	49√
5√	10√	15√	20	25	30	35	40√	45	50√

Companion Weaknesses (Dependent)

1√	6√	11√	16	21√	26√	31√	36	41√	46√
2√	7	12√	17√	22	27√	32√	37	42	47√
3√	8√	13√	18√	23	28√	33√	38√	43	48√
4√	9√	14√	19	24√	29√	34√	39√	44	49√
5√	10	15	20	25	30	35√	40√	45√	50√

SEVEN

Extremes and Excesses of Emotion

If I happened to run into a lion while strolling through my backyard, it wouldn't be surprising if I screamed at the top of my lungs and catapulted myself directly into a neighboring county. We'd all think it strange, however, if I had the same reaction to a gnat.

If we think that our world has caved in because someone didn't smile at us on the way to work or that someone hates us because they didn't call us last night, that's a bit strange, too. These last scenarios indicate extreme and excessive emotional reactions to ordinary events.

One of the characteristics of emotionally healthy individuals is that, in the course of our lives, we're able to experience reasonable emotional reactions to happenings in our environments. Yet, some of us have a tendency toward extreme emotional reactions to our environments.

Some of us, either by nature or due to our environment, are more intense than others. There's nothing wrong with that. On the other hand, if our emotional intensity is so extreme that it isolates us from others, or makes us so introspective that we can't cope with our environment, then that's a problem. This can occur when our intensity lingers and becomes a way of life rather than an occasional occurrence. The internal isolation resulting from such a situation can lead to depression.

Now let's look at another example. We've probably all experienced moments in our lives when we've been extremely happy with something, and have been eager to share our experiences. Yet, if that state of high excitement continued over a long period of time, the result would be fatigue, both for us and for all of those around us. Once again a state of isolation might result, as others grew weary of our extreme excitement.

So, while it's healthy to experience highs and lows, it's not healthy to live in the extremes of either.

The accounts that follow are of extreme or excessive emotional reactions to our environment that are unhealthy and detrimental to our lives.

I'm Not OK Unless You're OK With Me
Weakness: The Tendency to Be Defined by Others

I remember looking across the room one night at a restaurant where I was having dinner. Several tables away I noticed a beautiful woman who appeared to be at dinner with her husband and two children. My glance drifted into an empty stare as my thoughts began to return to my tasteful dinner.

When I came to consciousness I realized that I was stuck in an empty gaze. I could see that this woman thought that I was staring directly at her. In fact, it appeared that she thought that I must have seen something wrong with her hair. She kept looking at me, touching her hair, and then looking in a nearby mirror to adjust it. She'd then look back at me as if to see if what she'd done had met with my approval.

I looked away, somewhat embarrassed that I'd gotten my stare stuck on her hair, and resumed dinner, only to find myself quite curious about why she'd care what I, someone she didn't know, thought about how she looked.

My curiosity gnawed at me until I could take it no longer. I looked up again, but this time I stared at her right shoulder pad and frowned a bit. In seconds she was flicking at the top of her jacket over her right shoulder as if there were some evil lurking there. Again, she evaluated herself in the neighboring mirror. "Good grief!" I thought. "I have control over this woman from a distance of five dinner tables!"

I wondered if my power was omnipotent, so I tried the same tactic with others in the restaurant. I stared ferociously at some guy's bald spot, with no reaction. I stared at another woman's hair, again with no response. So, I returned to the woman whom I'd now have to call my victim and tried one more thing.

I looked at her son's jacket, which was slightly askew. Sure enough, she stealthily adjusted his jacket so that he was neat and tidy. I have no doubt that wherever I would've glanced, she'd have responded with some corrective action. It was easy to see from her meticulous, almost flawless appearance and from the similar appearance of the children that perfectionism was likely a part of the picture. Yet, I suspect that there may have been other forces at work as well under the surface.

Over the course of time, I repeated this experiment and found that this woman wasn't alone in her excessive sensitivity to what others thought of her. This seems to be a commonplace characteristic among teenagers, as they're vitally concerned with how they appear. We've probably all noticed how teenage boys change their walk if they become aware that we're looking at them. Somehow, they seem to instantly become tougher.

We expect this with teenagers to some degree, as they form their own concepts of themselves. Yet these excessive concerns with how others see us should be transient. They should come and go without great disturbance to our sense of self. They become a problem when they begin to dominate our thoughts, moods, or behaviors.

For some of us, our oversensitivity to what others think of us creates in us a more broad-based vulnerability that others don't experience. We're not OK unless others are OK with us. Somewhere along the way we've developed the weakness of taking our definition of who we are from others' opinions of us. Marissa is a good example here.

Marissa

Marissa had come to me fearing that her relationship of two years was disintegrating. Jeremy was having second thoughts about their relationship. He hadn't said it directly but Marissa recognized the signs.

"I can't stand the distance between us," she said. "I drive by his apartment just to be close to him."

I asked Marissa to tell me about the relationship.

"We can be so close at times," she said. "It's like we're just one person. When it's like that, everything is great. Then I'll see some expression on his face and I'll get scared. I'm afraid he's going to leave. He says he's not and gets on my case about reading things into his facial expressions. He says I'm driving him crazy. I just can't handle it if he's unhappy with me. I keep pressing him to tell me what's wrong. He says he can't stand all the pressure. Yet, I can't take it if he's unhappy with me."

It was clear that Marissa was not OK unless Jeremy was OK with her. She'd based how well she was doing on how he felt about her. Her definition of herself was a reflection of what he saw in her.

This type of dependency upon others for our sense of self places an impossible demand upon those we love. It means that they're responsible for our happiness and our well-being. Yet, our happiness and well-being are our own responsibility. If we ask those we love to fill this need, we doom them to failure. We're asking them to do the impossible.

What's the origin of this weakness of taking our definition of ourselves from the opinions of others?

Environmental oversensitivity. Some of us were so geared as children to the cues of our environment, the abuses in our lives, the tension in the home, the angry look on someone's face, that we learned to function from the outside in rather than from the inside out. If our spouse or our boyfriend is unhappy, so are we. This is Marissa's story.

Past hurts. We may have been seriously hurt in a past relationship, so that our sense of self was shattered. Now we look to others to rebuild our self-concept. We don't trust our own perceptions.

Dependency and failure to develop. We may have been raised by someone who made our decisions for us, or may be in relationship with someone who does that for us now. If so, we're likely to look to this person for our sense of who we are. We haven't developed our own sense of ourselves.

How do we overcome the weakness of being defined by others?

▶ *Take responsibility.* In the final analysis, each one of us is responsible for who we become. No one else can take credit for that, and we can't blame anyone else for it. We need to recognize this fact and take responsibility for our own development.

▶ *Take risks.* We need to take risks and be willing to make mistakes. We develop a sense of who we are by placing our thoughts and ideas out on the table and exposing ourselves intellectually and emotionally. When we differ with someone, we draw a line between us that clarifies who we are as individuals.

Marissa had to face the loneliness she felt at being alone. She came to understand that her dependence upon others for her self-worth and self-definition came from the empty feeling she had when she was alone. She realized that she didn't know who she was and she determined to find out. She pulled emotional and intellectual energy away from her weakness of being defined by others and invested it in having and expressing her own opinions and determining for herself what she believed. In the long run she developed strengths of courage, openness, and authenticity.

Companion Weaknesses

1√	6√	11	16	21√	26√	31	36	41√	46√
2	7	12√	17	22	27√	32√	37	42	47√
3√	8√	13	18√	23	28√	33	38√	43	48√
4√	9√	14√	19√	24	29	34√	39√	44	49√
5	10	15√	20	25	30√	35	40√	45√	50√

I Really Struggle With My Feelings
Weakness: The Tendency to Be Moody

During my high school years I had the privilege—or the misfortune, depending upon how you look at it—of participating in the state speech competition. I had an incredible crush on one of the boys who was going to the competition. I was excited to find that we'd be riding in the same car as we traveled to the big city. As a matter of fact, he was sitting right next to me. That would've been great, except that I was carsick the entire way there. I was so discouraged. Every few miles we had to stop, pull over, wait for my nausea to abate, and then take to the road again. And that was the best part of the trip.

While the secret object of my affections was presenting his speech, I dropped in to listen. He did poorly and left the room disappointed. I waited a few moments, got my courage up, and went out into the hallway to console him. I was excited to think that I might actually be able to help him deal with his disappointment. However, I was too late. Some little cheerleader type had found him and was carrying out my agenda.

My turn to compete came up and I listened to one brilliant master of words after another. This wasn't my idea of fun. So far as I could tell, there were no mistakes and the arguments were quite convincing. As much as I dreaded it, my time to speak finally arrived.

In the middle of my speech on nuclear disarmament, I forgot my speech. Out of reflex I slapped my hand on the podium, and as I did, I remembered the words to my speech. I stopped for a second, realized what I'd done, thought about throwing myself out of the window, and went on. When I finished my speech I sat down to the thundering applause of approximately one person. The rest were just plain confused about my style of presentation. So was I!

The other speakers presented their speeches as I sat there and ruminated on the absolute disaster of the entire trip. Being polite, I stayed to applaud the winners, but I really wanted to leave. First place was awarded, then second place, and I was preparing to leave as third place was being announced. I heard the judge say something about how he appreciated the passion with which the speech was presented, "especially when she hit the podium to emphasize her point," and then he called my name. I was shocked, a sentiment most of the people in the room shared, and embarrassed at the same time. Oh well, you just never know how things are going to work out.

I'd gone from excitement, to disappointment, to discouragement, to more discouragement, to shock, to embarrassment, and finally to relief, all within the confines of a single day. It was a lot to take, but this was an exceptional day. Not all of us are so lucky, however.

We all have our ups and downs, but some of us are consistently moody. Moodiness for us isn't an occasional experience but a state in which we live. Daniel was one who had to contend with moodiness.

Daniel

"What mood is she in?" This was the first question Daniel would ask his sister Jill upon his arrival home from school. Jill would ask the same question about her mother, should she be the one arriving home later.

It's not an uncommon question in homes or relationships where someone tends to be moody. The answer to this question gives those of us who ask it some sense of what to expect in the moments to come. It also gives us the information needed to prepare for an encounter with this person.

The need for this question robs those of us who ask it of the simplicity of life, a life of consistency and constancy. We live too often in a question mark, wondering what'll happen next. Anxiety becomes our constant companion. We learn to live in a perpetual state of preparedness, ready to deal with whatever mood we encounter, knowing that it may shift at any moment.

Daniel, now forty-two years old, sat with his wife, Breanne, in my office as she complained of having to walk on eggshells around him. She said that she could never tell what kind of mood he was going to be in, and that the situation was wearing her and the kids out. She was now living in the same type of environment that Daniel had experienced as a child.

Where does the weakness of moodiness originate?

Reaction to uncertainty. Moodiness causes those around the moody person to live in a state of uncertainty. Are we safe? Will things go smoothly? That uncertainty causes our moods to fluctuate. We then can become moody ourselves. Moodiness generates uncertainty. Uncertainty produces moodiness. This was David's story.

Others of us are overly sensitive to our environments or to what others think and that creates the uncertainty that produces moodiness. Furthermore, any tendencies toward being controlling, insecure, or dependent on any other human being can cause uncertainty and produce moodiness.

So how do we overcome the weakness of excessive moodiness?

▸ *Recognize and accept.* We need to recognize and accept that uncertainty is a natural part of life. It encourages us to question things and search for the truth.

▸ *Answer the question.* Never let a question go unanswered. Uncertainty is found in the refusal to accept an answer. If, at the end of questioning, uncertainty remains, then the answer is, "I don't know."

▸ *Have faith.* We need to be careful not to allow our sense of well-being to be based on any other human being or human endeavor. Here we must look to our faith and the object of our faith for our sense of well-being. Nowhere else can we find ultimate certainty.

When we're spiritually grounded, other strengths are developed and reinforced. Some of these strengths are character, truth, honesty, loyalty, selflessness, compassion, determination, leadership, responsible risk taking, and generosity.

Companion Weaknesses

1√	6√	11√	16	21	26	31√	36	41√	46√
2	7	12	17	22	27	32	37	42	47√
3√	8√	13√	18	23	28√	33√	38√	43	48√
4√	9√	14√	19	24	29	34√	39	44	49√
5√	10	15	20	25	30√	35√	40	45√	50√

Everything Seems So Futile
Weakness: Tendency Toward Depression

We all have our depressing moments, sometimes even hours or days. There was the year that I figured out there was no Santa Claus. I'm still not over that. I was also particularly disturbed when the Tooth Fairy retired and when *Cagney and Lacey* ended. What can I say, except that some things in life are particularly difficult to deal with?

Others may experience depression when the Dallas Cowboys lose or when the big trout gets away. For some, it may be triggered when they learn experientially that computers can catch a virus or that fireflies don't generate heat. Any way you look at it, life offers challenges. Some of them get us down. For most of us this is a transitory experience. For some, however, depression becomes a way of life.

If we look beyond the surface, we'll find that depression is, in fact, a serious state that requires understanding and great care. Christine is a good example of this.

Christine
Christine had that remote look on her face. Even when she talked and her face was animated, there was still something not quite right. It seemed to take effort for her to think, focus, and talk. It was as if there was some internal force pulling her emotionally downward.

It was subtle, but Christine was experiencing a slight depression. To her, it felt like a dark cloud was hanging over her emotions. She wouldn't have called it a depression, because she was able to function. She was able to laugh and feel good at times, especially when she was working. Yet, when she slowed down she felt emotional pain. It was a slight, almost indiscernible, pang of alienation but it was enough to make Christine's sense of normalcy different from that of others. In fact, Christine had never experienced what it was like to feel "normal," without that dark cloud or pang of alienation. Hers was a type of depression most often identified by others first.

Christine was raised in a relatively stable home where there was a mild amount of arguing between her parents. Christine, being an exceptionally sensitive child, took the arguing to be more serious than it actually was. She'd hide in her room and wait until they stopped arguing to come out. Fear of her parents divorcing was almost always in the back of her mind. She obsessed on what would happen to her if they divorced. Much of what she did was done with fear of divorce as her emotional backdrop. She studied hard in school, thinking she'd have to get a scholarship because divorced parents couldn't pay for her education. She stayed out of trouble, thinking that she might contribute to the divorce.

Christine's parents never divorced, but Christine lived a life of worry and fear, leading to the subjective experience of depression. She lived life at a lower level of satisfaction than most, and a higher level of disappointment. She had learned to live at the survival level, and this robbed her of the joy of life.

What's the origin of this weakness of depression?

Sensitivity to our environment. Certainly there are circumstances in our lives that cause us sadness and may warrant periods of depression. We may suffer loss and pain. Yet there are other reasons for depression. As an example, our level of sensitivity may contribute to depression.

Each of us has a different level of sensitivity in any given area of life. Those who become doctors are able to look at a wound and deal with it while others might faint. Those with red hair have been shown by research to be more physically sensitive to pain than those with other hair colors. Some of us are more emotionally sensitive than others. Sensitivity is a wonderful thing but oversensitivity can be debilitating.

Emotional attenuation. If we're subjected to a tension-filled environment for an extended period of time, our emotions may be affected. They may be dampened to accommodate sadness and worry or heightened to accommodate anxiety and fear. Our emotions may remain at these abnormal levels long after we leave the stressful environment, and these emotional extremes can lead to depression.

Extreme or crisis-oriented thinking. Our state of reactivity or sensitivity to our environments is influenced by our perspective. If our thoughts tend to be extreme or crisis-oriented, we're more likely to struggle with depression. If we think that something is horrible it'll make us feel a lot worse than if we think that it's simply uncomfortable or difficult. Since our emotions follow our thoughts and words, how we think can seriously contribute to depression.

How, then, can we overcome the weakness of depression?

▶ *Seek truth.* We must conform our lives to current truth. Though in the past it may have made sense to feel depressed, we must seek to determine whether depression is a proper response to our current reality, and then we must take steps, such as seeking therapy and medication, to get ourselves out of that state.

▶ *Recognize our own power.* As children we may have been helpless to change our circumstances or to stop the trauma. We may have suffered because we weren't big enough or mature enough to do anything about the situation. As adults we may still find ourselves paralyzed by feelings of helplessness and fear. We must recognize that as adults we're no longer helpless and we don't need to be afraid. We have the power to change our lives. We must choose the current truth or our lives will be governed by the past.

▶ *Conform our words to reality.* If we've developed the tendency to communicate either with ourselves or with others using extreme or crisis-oriented words, we're not likely to be living according to reality. We must evaluate our communication to be sure that what we say is accurate. We need to capture each word and hammer it into submission to the truth. If something is uncomfortable, we don't need to say that it's awful. We should say that something hurts and that it's going to take some time to recover rather than saying that it's unbearable. If something happens at all, we must not say that it never happens. We must accept responsibility for our contribution to our own depression and change what's within our power.

Christine had taught herself to be reactive and overly sensitive to her environment. She'd trained her thoughts and emotions to be negative and hurtful. Understanding what she'd done and that she could do it differently, she began to make changes. As she withdrew her emotional and intellectual energy from her weakness of depression and redirected it into living according to the current truth, strengths began to develop. She began to grow in the areas of truth, self-discipline, self-respect, personal responsibility, clear and accurate thinking, and emotional and intellectual freedom.

Companion Weaknesses

1√	6√	11	16	21√	26√	31	36	41√	46
2√	7√	12	17	22	27√	32√	37	42	47√
3√	8√	13	18√	23	28√	33	38√	43	48
4√	9√	14√	19	24	29	34√	39√	44	49
5√	10	15	20√	25	30√	35√	40	45	50√

I Take Things Personally
Weakness: The Tendency to Personalize

When I was a young girl, I was crazy about Ricky Nelson. It was such a private thing, just me and a few million other young girls. When he sang, I was sure it was to me, even though the title of the song was "Hello Mary Lou." I wasn't jealous of all of the other girls he referred to in "Travelin' Man." I told myself it was just a song. I walked around with him in "Lonesome Town." "Fools Rush In" and "For You" were just for me, of course. Ahh ... there's nothing quite like the teenage imagination!

When it came to Ricky Nelson, I lived in a wonderful dream. It was all about me. It was interesting to me to find that years later when I heard "Garden Party" I could still hear the Ricky Nelson I'd been so crazy about. The difference was that I'd grown up and could now listen to his voice for its own quality instead of making it personal, all about me.

Some of us go beyond teenage self-absorption. We think that most of what happens in our environment is about us, even to the state of discomfort. We personalize things. Let me give you an example.

Someone might ask us, "Why did you go to that movie?" It's a simple question. Most of us will interpret this question as asking us why we liked a particular movie. We'll respond with a comment like, "I went because I like the actors," or, "Because I like the plot." Yet others of us will interpret this question to mean that we're being criticized or doubted. We'll respond to the question defensively, with questions of our own: "Why? Did I do something wrong? Are you upset with me because I went to that movie? Why shouldn't I go to that movie? Why are you so critical of me?"

This second set of responses is characteristic of those of us who personalize. We take things that aren't meant personally as if they were. Michael is an example of someone with this weakness.

Michael

"I can't say anything to him," Michael's wife, Margaret, said. "He gets so defensive."

"It's how you say it," Michael retorted. "I wouldn't get so defensive if you wouldn't say things the way you do."

"Please help me understand why you get so angry with me," Margaret gently requested.

"I don't get it! You act like you don't get angry at all!" Michael shot back. "Why don't we talk about your anger for a while?"

"Honey, I'm willing to talk about my anger, but I'm concerned about what's happening to the children when you yell at them so often," she said.

"I don't abuse our children. I never hit them. I resent you painting this picture of me," Michael said. "You just want to take them away from me!"

"I never said you hit the children!" Margaret protested. "And I don't want to take them away from you."

I listened to them talk and didn't hear anything in Margaret's communication that was in any way an attack on Michael. Yet that's the way he heard it. Michael was demonstrating the hallmarks of personalizing. He was reading things that weren't there into what Margaret was saying, and his bias on those things was negative. He was also reactive to her statements and defensive, getting upset for reasons that didn't make sense. What was going on with this conversation and why?

Where does this weakness of personalizing originate?

Arrogance. Some of us just think the world revolves around us. Others of us use arrogance as a cover for insecurity. Either one may lead to personalizing, but when it relates to insecurity the personalizing is typically negative.

Negative self-concept. Michael thought so little of himself that he assumed that others felt that way too. He was looking for rejection in almost everything they said. He struck out at any hint of criticism and felt judged by any difference of opinion. He had learned in his childhood that he needed to protect himself from any further negative appraisal. His father had often called him an idiot, saying that he would never amount to anything. The pain of the constant diminishing statements left Michael with no room for any further criticism. Emotionally he was filled to capacity with rejection by someone who was supposed to have loved him. Margaret was having trouble getting through all of the defenses. She expressed discontent with some of Michael's behavior but he heard it as a criticism of who he was as a person.

The perceived need for self-protection. If we're in a traumatic environment for an extended period of time, we tend to become highly self-protective. We see everything around us as potentially harmful to us. We necessarily focus on ourselves and on the environment around us in regard to us. When we leave this type of environment, we may still feel at risk to what is around us. Everything around us is seen as being about us.

Those of us who have experienced turbulent or emotionally charged childhoods tend to take things more personally. If we walk into a room where others are quietly speaking, we may wonder if they're speaking secretly about us. If we're in a group of people and someone asks, "Who left the lid off the catsup?" we may automatically feel guilty, even if we haven't been near the catsup bottle. If the choir director complains that someone is off-key we worry that we're the one. When the police drive down the highway and turn their siren on, we think they are following us. This happens because our focus, either as a child or in some later oppressive environment, was on surviving. We focused solely on how things affected us. This focus will continue until we can come to understand why it's there and accept that we've developed the weakness of tending to take things personally.

So, how can we overcome the weakness of personalizing?

▶ *Recognize our weakness.* We must first face the fact that we do personalize things, and must begin to seek the underlying reasons for this weakness.

▶ *Seek the truth.* Then, we must respond with truth to the things we say to ourselves and begin to accept the truth about us rather than what we negatively suspect about ourselves. If we think that someone is talking about us, we need to listen and see whether this is true. Once we see that it generally isn't true, we'll stop wondering about it. If we feel guilty about something, we must stop and respond to that guilt. "Did I use the catsup today? No. Then it wasn't me who left the lid off. Do I sing off-key? No. Are the police after me? No." We must train ourselves to live in the current reality, and must continually challenge our own negative self-accusations.

When Michael put these suggestions into practice, he began to separate himself from the past. His relationship with his wife improved and he began to develop strengths in the areas of truth, building relationships, openness, self-respect, and sound thinking.

Companion Weaknesses

1√	6√	11√	16	21√	26√	31√	36	41√	46√
2	7√	12√	17√	22	27√	32√	37	42	47√
3√	8√	13√	18√	23	28√	33	38√	43	48√
4√	9	14√	19√	24	29	34√	39√	44	49√
5√	10	15√	20	25√	30	35	40√	45√	50√

I'm Guilt-Prone
Weakness: Condemning Conscience

There have been a few moments in my life when I've gotten a glimpse of the diabolical side of myself. OK, there have been more than just a few. This one, I admit, I truly enjoyed.

It was a Sunday morning and I had just finished teaching a Bible study. I left one building, headed for the main sanctuary, and looked back at the parking lot to see if my new car was still there. It was the first new car I'd ever owned and I was quite excited about it. It was one of the first cars with a remote device that would unlock the doors from a distance.

As I was looking out at the parking lot I saw a woman and her little boy just about to walk past my new car. Well, enter the dark side. Just as they were passing the rear part of the car, I pushed the remote control and the trunk flew open, startling them both. Let me just go ahead and admit that I should have been shot for such a thing. At church, too!

What was particularly interesting to me was that a split second later the little boy automatically and with great vigor threw his hands into the air, looked absolutely petrified, turned immediately to his mother, and said "I didn't do it!" Ironically, at the very same time, his mother automatically turned and glared at him as if he'd done something wrong!

I was at the car within another two seconds, explaining my own bad behavior and apologizing. I felt guilty, and I should have. Appropriate guilt is a good thing, intended for our welfare. It let me know that I was out of line. We all had a good laugh and I promised myself I'd behave ... for a while. I knew better than to have excessively high expectations of myself.

Some of us, like the little boy, occasionally feel guilty when we have no reason to. Yet, others of us live with a nearly constant, uneasy sense of guilt. Our consciences continually condemn us, without proper reason. Doris is an example of this type of thinking.

Doris

In the midst of a discussion, I accidentally knocked a coaster off of the coffee table in front of Doris.

"I'm sorry!" she said.

"Oh," I said. "It wasn't your fault. It was mine." I took a few seconds to gather up the coaster and then asked Doris, "Do you always apologize for things you didn't do?"

"Yes, I do." she said. "I don't know why, but I do."

There are several reasons why we might apologize when we have done nothing wrong. Sometimes it's our way of avoiding conflict and controlling the situation. If we apologize quickly then the conflict is over. The issue isn't resolved but the conflict is over. Sometimes we fear harmful repercussions if we don't apologize. Some of us do it because we're guilt-prone.

Chronic apologizing is common among those of us who are guilt-prone. The instant something goes wrong, we figure it's our fault. We've developed condemning consciences. Why is that?

Where does the weakness of a condemning conscience originate?

We may have been the subject of frequent or harsh criticism. When that happens, we begin to anticipate being wrong, even if we aren't. Here our consciences have conformed to the accusations against us. We then become the accusers ourselves.

We may have faced the pressure of unreasonable, excessive, or harsh standards. Here we find the perfectionists, who are as much a tyrant to themselves as they are to others. Those of us who are legalists fit in here, too. We live according to the letter of the law without regard to our own or others' tender spirits. We've mistakenly incorporated into our conscience rules and regulations that are brutal and without mercy. We don't avoid doing what's wrong because we love what's right; we avoid doing what's wrong because we live in fear of punishment.

So how can this weakness be overcome?

▶ *Change the question.* When something goes wrong, those of us who are guilt-prone immediately ask ourselves what we did wrong. Why do we do this? Did someone accuse us? If no one has told us that, we should not assume it. We need to change our instinctive question into an observation.

For instance, if a friend seems quiet, instead of asking, "Did I do something wrong?" we might say something like, "You seem a little down today. If you want to talk, just let me know." This observation doesn't assume that we've caused the problem, but it doesn't avoid the problem, either.

▶ *Take a "wait and see" approach to the situation.* Instead of assuming the worst, we need to wait for clarification. We must avoid filling in the blanks with negative assumptions and suspicions. Instead, we need to simply refuse to think about it until someone indicates verbally that there's more to talk about.

▶ *Challenge the guilty feeling.* If we feel guilty we need to ask, "What am I guilty of?" This is what Doris learned to do. She was extremely guilt-prone, partly in response to having a critical mother. Doris would go to visit her mother and soon would be feeling guilty. She would think, "Why is she so grumpy with me? What did I do wrong this time? Oh no, I must have said or done something."

Doris was responding to her condemning conscience by anticipating that it was right and that she'd done wrong. Since all of this was going on in her head, there was no objective way for her to determine the truth. When we experience feelings of guilt, we need to challenge those feelings. When internal questions arise, we must strive to answer them honestly. "I don't know why she's grumpy and I'm not going to assume it's about me. She can let me know if there's a problem. I have no awareness of having done anything wrong. I don't need to worry. This may not have anything to do with me."

Doris began to adjust her conscience to reflect reality. By not assuming what she didn't know, she stopped causing herself so much internal stress. In the process of redirecting her emotional and intellectual energies away from false guilt, Doris developed strengths in the areas of truth, accurate self-appraisal, respect for herself and others, and patience.

Companion Weaknesses

1√	6√	11	16	21√	26	31√	36√	41√	46
2	7√	12√	17	22	27	32√	37	42	47
3√	8√	13	18√	23√	28	33√	38√	43	48
4√	9	14√	19	24	29	34√	39√	44	49
5	10	15	20√	25	30	35	40	45	50√

EIGHT

Confusion

Some time back I lived in an apartment complex. I don't know why they called it a complex. It was really quite simple. However, I guess that's a topic of investigation for another time. Anyway, as I left my apartment one afternoon, I noticed a fancy two-way walkie-talkie sitting on a nearby ledge. Having a yen for gadgets, I picked it up and examined it, never giving one wit of consideration to the fact that, had it been a bomb, I might have been blown to smithereens!

I knew enough about Dick Tracy to know what it was, so I pushed down on the lever that let two-way communication commence, lowered my voice, and said, "Ground control to Major Tom.... This is ground control to Major Tom." Then I made that sound that cell phones make when they're breaking up and repeated the message. "Ground control to Major Tom.... This is ground control to Major Tom." Then I let go of the lever and secretly giggled myself half to death.

At that point, I knew two things. Somewhere, some guy was looking for his expensive walkie-talkie. And, somewhere else, his boss and anyone else around him was listening to someone on the walkie-talkie saying "Ground control to Major Tom ... This is ground control to Major Tom." I loved it!

When I decided that I'd done enough mischief, a hard line for me to negotiate, I took the walkie-talkie to the apartment complex management office. There, standing around a walkie-talkie, was a group of people waiting for another message from outer space! What a laugh we all had, except for the guy who'd lost the walkie-talkie. Oh well, you can't please everyone.

Life can certainly be confusing at times, and we don't need to make it more confusing. Yet we do it anyway. We confuse ourselves about ourselves. We also confuse others about us. Here are five ways in which we accomplish this feat.

I Feel Like a Fraud
Weakness: Discomfort With Accepting Compliments

If someone came up to me and told me how wonderful they thought I was in the film version of "Mary Queen Of Scots," I'd probably feel pretty uncomfortable. That would mainly be because I've never been in a movie. If the compliment were about something for which I could legitimately take the credit, I'd feel more comfortable with it. Accepting compliments is a wonderful privilege, but some of us don't feel that good about doing it.

The Singer Guy
Have you ever heard someone sing with a voice that just carried you away? What a wonderful experience. I thank God that people with gifts like these use them. Some time ago I attended an event where I had the pleasure of hearing a beautiful tenor solo. After the event I expressed my gratitude to the gentleman who'd entertained us for his wonderful song and for sharing his beautiful voice with us.

"It wasn't me," he said. "It was God."

I very much appreciated his sentiment and inwardly agreed with him. Yet, while I wanted to appreciate the marvelous gift that God had given this man, I wanted to appreciate him as well. So, I responded to his statement.

"It sounded like you," I said.

"Pardon me?" he queried with his ear bent toward me as he tried to understand.

"I said it sounded like you. The song, it sounded like you were singing it," I said, knowing I was about to tweak his thinking.

"I just want God to get the glory, not me," he said with a smile.

"I'm sure he did," I said, "but I wanted you to feel appreciated too. You could have chosen not to sing. Yet, you did sing, and I appreciate it. I just didn't want to bypass you in all of this. Obviously, God used you. You weren't invisible. I don't want to pretend I didn't see you or appreciate you. I hope you don't mind."

"Not at all," he said. "Thank you for putting it that way."

Our paths didn't cross again for several years, which was probably fortunate for him. Then, we met again. This time he started the conversation.

"I wanted to tell you," he started, "that I thought quite a bit about what you said to me the first time we met. What you said kept gnawing at my brain and wouldn't leave me alone." He told me he knew I was a therapist, so he figured I was talking to him in some kind of code. How right he was. He recognized from our conversation that he had difficulty accepting compliments.

"I was frustrated with you for trying to make me accept a compliment," he said.

"Did you realize the scope of what you were doing?" I asked.

"Not right at first," he said, "but boy, did I after I thought about it, and I appreciate you for bringing it to my attention."

"Unlike some people, I accept your compliment!" I kidded him.

What he'd realized was that he was using God to cover for his insecurities. It sounded righteous and noble to refer everything back onto God, and he did sincerely want God to be glorified, as I'm sure he was. Yet, without realizing it, he was avoiding dealing with his own sense of unworthiness. Because of that, he was missing out on all of the joy that belonged to him.

Where does the weakness of discomfort with accepting compliments originate?

A low sense of self-worth. Some of us, like this gentleman, are uncomfortable with compliments because we don't feel deserving. We've been told so often that we're not good enough that we now believe it. When we're complimented we act pleased, yet feel like frauds.

Avoidance of pride. Others of us can't accept compliments because we feel that it will lead to pride, which a bad thing. Yet, the Bible itself tells us to encourage one another. So, what happens to encouragers if we don't let them use the gifts God has given them?

How can we overcome the weakness of discomfort with accepting compliments?

▶ *Analyze.* If we struggle with accepting compliments, we need to ask ourselves what experiences or beliefs are prompting the discomfort. Only after we've recognized the underlying causes of our discomfort can we begin to work to overcome them.

▶ *Seek the current truth.* We then need to determine what really makes sense, with our current situation. For example, if as a child we were treated in such a way that we began to feel unworthy, we need to ask ourselves if that feeling makes sense in our current situation. If we've been taught that accepting compliments is a dangerous and prideful thing, we need to compare that teaching to our current truth. Are we truly in danger of becoming prideful? If not, then this is a false notion, and should be discarded.

▶ *Recognize our own worth.* We need to understand that we're valuable and worthy of reasonable recognition and encouragement. If we can accept this fact we'll be well on the way to overcoming the weakness of discomfort with compliments.

If we'll challenge our discomfort with accepting compliments, as this wonderful singer did, we'll uncover any hidden insecurities. Once we've dealt with them we'll find we've developed strengths of accurate self-perception, authenticity, and honesty.

Companion Weaknesses

1√	6√	11	16	21√	26√	31√	36	41	46
2√	7√	12√	17	22	27	32	37	42	47√
3√	8√	13√	18√	23	28√	33	38√	43	48
4√	9	14√	19√	24	29	34√	39√	44√	49√
5√	10	15√	20√	25	30	35√	40	45√	50√

I Feel Like I Don't Belong
Weakness: Failure to Integrate Personal Differences

Do you remember junior high school, that place and time when the opinions of peers weighed more than most anything else? It was a place where the intense need to belong reigned supreme. It was also the scene of some of my most embarrassing moments.

My junior high school class was having an end-of-the-year swimming party and, like all of the other girls in the class, I wanted to sport the new creation known as the two-piece bathing suit. (Yes, I'm very, very old!)

At the community center I changed into my new bathing suit and headed for the pool. I stood at the edge of the pool, looking out over my friends, only to find them staring back at me. It seemed that the abundance of ruffles sewn on my suit left me standing there looking like a topiary—you know, one of those bouffant poodle trees.

I disappeared into the water faster than Houdini could have gotten me there, and my reputation for coolness disappeared equally as fast. I stayed in the pool until my friends were gone, trying to act nonchalant while my skin shriveled underneath a rotisserie-style sunburn. For what seemed like an eternity that day, I felt that I no longer belonged with the crowd in the way I had before—no longer a leader, just a topiary.

My sense of coolness did eventually return, because I threatened instant pain to anyone who ever brought up the bouffant poodle incident again, yet I can still remember the painful feelings I experienced that day.

We all have our moments of feeling like we don't belong, a sense of being uncomfortably different. Yet, these are generally transient experiences, soon replaced by other, more comfortable, sensations. For some of us, however, the feeling of not belonging never really lets up. It becomes a weakness that haunts us and keeps us from feeling secure and at home in life. That's how it was with Peggy.

Peggy

Peggy sat in front of me with a look of agony on her face. She complained of feeling alone, of being misunderstood, and of being rejected by the people about whom she cared. She felt used and hurt.

"It's been like this all my life," she said. "What's wrong with me? What am I doing wrong? Why won't they let me in?"

Peggy was confused and broken. She'd never felt like she fit in. She'd never had a sense of belonging. It hurt to watch her hurt.

What was going on?

Troubled background. If we've come from traumatic or troubled environments or have experienced excessively traumatic events in our lives, we may have difficulty fitting in. We may not think like others do, or relate in the same way that they do. We may feel advanced, different, or misunderstood. People may not understand our intensity, and may think there's something wrong with us. We might prefer that we were just like everyone else, but we weren't given that option. The differences that we've acquired while learning to survive our troubled environments may then alienate us from our next social world, the one outside of the family. The effects of traumatic backgrounds don't stop at the front door when we leave home. This was Peggy's story.

Because we become caretakers, we give more than others and are aware of not getting as much back. We think this is because others don't care as much as we do, but it's because we're overdeveloped. We're conditioned to overgive, and we can do it instantly and at great depth. Others aren't incapable; we've just had more practice. We've already gone beyond where other people go. We experience more internal analysis, and with every step we take, we further limit the number of those who can understand or relate to us.

We don't understand that we're experiencing personal differences. There's nothing wrong with any of us. We just come from different types of environments and we don't know how to relate to each other. The mistake we make is taking this personally. When we do, we fail to integrate personal differences into our thinking.

On the other end of the coin are those of us who leave our traumatic environments to find that we're underdeveloped or socially broken in other ways. We're angry and don't know it. We're excessively afraid of rejection. We have excessive needs for approval. We look to others to define us because we're unsure of ourselves. Then we walk out into a world that was never intended to compensate for those flaws. Again, we feel that we don't belong. Then we blame others for not accepting us. Yet they're at as much of a disadvantage as we are. We're as different and difficult for them to understand as they are for us.

So, how can we get conquer the weakness of not integrating personal differences?

▶ *Let go of the need to know it all.* In order to begin to fit in, those of us who come from troubled backgrounds will have to make changes in some things that seem basic to us. Because of our concentration on survival, whether emotional or physical, we overanalyze everything. That's a part of what makes us feel that we don't belong.

In our troubled pasts, the only way we could feel safe was if we were aware of everything that was going on around us. We had to continually be thinking ahead in order to protect ourselves from every bad thing that could happen. Even when we're no longer in an environment that requires it, we still have the tendency to overthink everything. We're like giant thrashing machines that farmers use to suck in the hay and grind it into mulch. We suck all of the thoughts and possibilities out of the universe and grind them up in our brains until they become indiscernible from one another.

It's hard and sometimes painful for us to say "I don't know." Yet that's precisely what we need to learn to accept and to say. It's OK for us not to know everything.

▶ *Accept ourselves.* Many of us absolutely refuse to accept ourselves as we are. Because we're uncomfortable with our differences from others, we spend our time trying to change either them or ourselves so that we'll be the same. Yet, we're not supposed to be the same. We need to allow and accept differences. We need to learn to appreciate them. Only then will we become comfortable with them.

When Peggy considered all of these things, she began to change her thinking. Instead of investing in the pain of difference and the disappointment of others not being the way she wanted them to be, she chose to accept them as they were. The pressure on her to control her environment began to dissipate and she began to relax. In time, she developed strengths in the areas of acceptance of and respect for others, patience, and humility. When she stopped trying to force others to conform to her world, she found that she belonged in theirs.

Companion Weaknesses

1√	6√	11√	16√	21√	26√	31√	36√	41√	46√
2√	7	12√	17√	22	27√	32√	37	42√	47√
3√	8√	13√	18√	23	28√	33√	38√	43	48
4√	9√	14√	19√	24	29	34√	39√	44√	49√
5√	10	15√	20√	25√	30√	35√	40√	45√	50√

I Don't Trust People
Weakness: The Tendency Toward Distortions in Perceptions

Have you ever gone back as an adult to visit somewhere you lived when you were young, only to find that things had changed? The house you lived in is smaller. The ice cream at the dairy isn't quite as creamy. The burgers at the drive-thru are smaller. It's not so much that "You can't go home again"; it's just that it's a lot smaller when you get there. Why is that?

Many of us experience distortions in our perceptions. We look at something in our present through the lens of an old memory that doesn't match current reality. This is what happened to Joe. He couldn't seem to separate out past truth from current truth, and this was destroying his life and relationships.

Joe

Joe lived in a state of extreme distress, and so did those around him. He completely dominated his wife. She had to account to him for every phone call she'd made and what she'd said in all of them. He would grill her constantly with questions and accusations about the happenings of her every day. Why did he do this? Why did he see her as untrustworthy when she was doing nothing wrong? Where does this weakness of distorted perceptions originate?

Incorrect information. We may have distorted perceptions because we've listened to the wrong information. There was a time when lots of people were convinced that the world was flat. More often than not, our distorted thinking comes from looking at life through the lens of some other space and time.

This was Joe's first marriage, but it wasn't his first relationship. He'd previously been in a two-year relationship with a woman who was unfaithful. Joe was using all kinds of abusive methods to assure that it wouldn't happen again. He had no right to treat his wife this way, but her rights weren't as important to him as his need to protect himself. This is an unfortunate distorted perspective shared by many who have been hurt. We think that our need to protect ourselves justifies any and all of our behavior. Yet, it doesn't. Not only do we have distortions in our perceptions of others, but in our perceptions of ourselves as well.

Joe could see only what he was afraid of. If he allowed himself to see the truth—that his wife loved him and was faithful—he would be at risk of letting down his protective guard, so he wouldn't allow himself to see the whole truth. Nothing his wife did was going to change that. His distrust of her was his way of staying safe. He'd trapped both of them and left no way out. This is why controlling situations can become so volatile and frightening.

We need to remind ourselves of something here. Joe was struggling with a weakness. He had the power to change it. For him, the question was not whether he could, but whether he would. From his perspective, even though he was destroying his life and the lives of others, at least he was making sure that his wife wasn't being unfaithful to him. In this respect, things were working well.

When we think with distorted perceptions, the hardest thing we have to do is develop a willingness to relinquish them. It sounds easy doesn't it? Yet, in the beginning, it's about as easy as pulling a submerged elephant out of a tar pit, by its nose, by yourself ... in the wintertime.

So how do we overcome the weakness of distorted perceptions?

▶ *Challenge the truthfulness of our perceptions.* One reason that relinquishing distorted perceptions is so difficult is that we often believe these distorted perceptions to be true. We need to challenge this assumption. The best way to do this is to develop a list of questions that'll reveal the truth about the current situation without regard to other situations. We need to see today without being under the influence of yesterday.

Here were some of Joe's questions and the answers: Has my wife ever been unfaithful to me? No. Has she ever given me the slightest indication that she'd be unfaithful to me? No. Do I have any reason, given to me by her, that I should fear her being unfaithful? No.

We have to eliminate the temptation to say "no, but" at the end of all of these answers. In that way we resist the temptation to spread our negative bias of the past into the future. Every time Joe put a "no, but" at the end of one of these answers, I asked him to go back and answer the question again, taking into account only the current situation, until it finally sank in. It was a long, long session. I was really proud of Joe because not all of us with distorted perceptions are willing to change them. We choose to stay in our own self-created prisons, and we try to get others to stay there, too.

▶ *Determine the purpose our distorted perceptions serve.* The second reason distorted perceptions are so difficult to change is because they often come to serve some specific purpose in our lives. In order to get rid of them, we have to reconsider that purpose and determine whether it still makes sense today. If it does, then we need to figure out some other way to deal with it that is respectful to all involved. If that purpose no longer makes sense, then we need to release it. Joe had no reason to hold on to his distorted perceptions.

What Joe did took a great deal of courage. He is a clear demonstration that it is possible to stop distorted thinking and the abusive behavior that accompanies it. In time, Joe developed strengths in personal responsibility, trust, honesty, truth, and leadership.

The companion weaknesses checked in the following are those that would most commonly accompany distorted perceptions related to trust, such as those Joe experienced. Companion weaknesses may vary with other types of distorted perceptions.

Companion Weaknesses

1√	6√	11√	16√	21√	26√	31√	36	41√	46√
2√	7√	12√	17√	22	27√	32√	37√	42√	47√
3√	8√	13√	18√	23	28√	33√	38	43	48√
4√	9√	14	19√	24√	29	34√	39	44	49√
5√	10	15√	20	25√	30√	35	40√	45√	50√

I Live in the Land of Mixed Messages
Weakness: Excessive Caution and Fear of Exposure

You can always tell, down South, when someone is giving you the wrong directions. You ask if they'll give you directions to the grocery store and they tell you "Showa (that's sure spelled southern), you just go right on down to the bridge, not the first one, the second bridge. So, you go past the first bridge and then the second bridge until you get to the third bridge. Then you go past the third bridge until you get to the mailbox with the rooster on it, not the yellow rooster because that's about a mile further. You go to the mailbox with the red rooster on it. You know ... those metal roosters. Not a real one. If you see a real rooster on a mailbox, you just keep right on going until you get to the mailbox with the red metal rooster on it. Then you go past two red brick houses to Sandy Side Road. Well, I'm not showa now, because they rezoned and they changed the name of that street. Now let me see here, what is the name of that street ..." If you haven't succumbed to brain death by the time they're through, you get to experience the *coup de grâce*. They grin. There it is, a perfect and experiential example of a mixed message. Someone is smiling in your face as they send you to Mars.

Mixed messages at their best are confusing. At their worst they're dishonest places to hide. Russ is a good example.

Russ

Russ moved from relationship to relationship. The women's complaints were almost always the same. They complained that he wouldn't come right out and say that the relationship was a committed one. He wouldn't refer to any of these women as his girlfriend. He wouldn't take them out with his friends. Most of the time, he'd rather go over to their places, have dinner, and hang out. On the rare occasions when he would have a woman over to his house, he'd turn his telephone off and let voice mail take the calls. Eventually, he would become a bit more comfortable with a woman and while away on a trip he'd ask her to water the plants or feed the dog. He'd slip and leave his phone on and she'd answer it. It would be another woman friend, who would be surprised to hear another woman answer the phone.

All of these women felt like they were close to Russ. They all felt like they were the special one, even though he'd been clear with them early on that he wasn't ready to settle down. Unfortunately, he also told each of them that she was just the kind of woman he'd like to marry. That mixed message kept them hanging on.

What is the origin of mixed messages?

Fear. More often than not, mixed messages result from the weaknesses of fear of exposure and the excessive caution that comes with it. If the fear persists long enough it becomes a weakness that pervades all areas of our lives. It becomes a motivation for control.

Control. When we don't trust people or when being open and honest will bring repercussions we don't want, we may develop a pattern of vagueness in our communication. Others might call us secretive. We call it privacy. It's actually control. Our ability to trust has been damaged or is underdeveloped and we sense the need to protect ourselves.

We edit what we say to avoid being tied down, to avoid being known too well. Trying to tie us down to something definitive can be like trying to catch air in a butterfly net. We're experts at being elusive.

There's a part of us that knows we're trying to deliberately deceive. Yet, it's survival and that prompts us and justifies our behavior. We feel safer behind the opaque and the oblique. We let others know only what we would have them know.

Our tendency to protect ourselves in this way produces severe frustration in those who wish to know us and those who love us, because they aren't allowed to really get to know us. They're trapped in the tyranny of the vague. Over time, our mastery of nondisclosure serves to help us avoid not only pain but responsibility and change as well. This costs us discipline, growth, and relationships.

How can the weakness of fear of exposure be overcome?

▶ *Question.* The only way out is to catch ourselves editing our responses and ask ourselves why we're doing this. Then we need to ask ourselves whether this type of self-protection is really necessary.

▶ *Speak out.* If the protection is not reasonable, then we need to say what we really think and learn to handle the normal repercussions we'll experience in life.

▶ *Re-evaluate.* If we feel there really is a need to protect ourselves, then we need to re-evaluate the current relationship and bring it into conformity with honesty and emotional safety.

Russ robbed his weakness of his time and energy and instead became an honest man. He realized that he was trying to keep the doors open to his relationships and in doing so was being dishonest and compromising his character. He realized that he'd fooled even himself into thinking he was being honest with women, but he wasn't. In the long run Russ developed strengths in the areas of truth, leadership, honesty, openness, character, personal responsibility, and spiritual life.

Companion Weaknesses

1√	6√	11√	16	21√	26	31	36	41√	46√
2√	7√	12√	17	22	27	32√	37	42√	47√
3√	8√	13√	18	23	28	33√	38√	43√	48
4√	9	14√	19	24√	29	34	39	44	49√
5√	10	15√	20	25	30	35	40√	45	50√

Everybody Is Out to Get Me
Weakness: Protective Paranoia

Some time back I worked for a company that was putting together a big marketing and sales program. I went with a co-worker into my manager's office and presented some ideas I'd put together for the campaign. The manager acted lukewarm about my ideas, so we left his office and went back to our desks. I put my presentation materials back into my briefcase, closed it, and left it sitting on my desk. My co-worker and I were on our way out of the office to a meeting when I asked her to turn around and go back with me to our department. We slowed down and very carefully looked around the corner toward my desk. There at my desk, rifling through my briefcase, was my manager.

The sight of my manager trying to pilfer my ideas shocked my co-worker, but it didn't shock me. I'd had stuff like that happen before, and his overt behaviors were obviously questionable. If our trust is repeatedly violated, we can begin to believe that others are out to get us. We may develop the weakness of protective paranoia. That's what happened with Mack.

Mack
Mack was at war with one of his neighbors. His neighbor was putting up a fence, and Mack swore that the neighbor was annexing some of his land. Mack would go out when he knew his neighbor wasn't home

and measure the fence and the distance to his driveway. You'd have thought he was the CIA with all his cloak-and-dagger tactics.

According to his wife, this wasn't new for Mack. He was sure the department store salesman had changed the price on the refrigerator he'd bought. He was afraid that the movers who had come to take the old couch were going to steal his spare watches. What was this all about?

What are the origins of this "everybody's out to get me" thinking?

Previous harm. With Mack it was simple. He'd been burglarized before, and ever since then he'd been paranoid about it happening again. I say paranoid because Mack no longer lives in such a vulnerable environment. Furthermore, Mack had taken his fear beyond someone taking his household things to seeing people in conspiracies to take other things from him.

It's one thing to be concerned about one neighborhood or one person and the potential harm there. It's quite another thing, however, to think that every neighborhood is terribly unsafe or that everyone is out to get us.

Modeling. We may have had a parent who was constantly suspicious of his or her spouse, and we may have subscribed to the notion that spouses aren't to be trusted. The same thing holds true in other contexts, such as suspicion of the government, the church, etc. We may share the paranoia.

Environment. We may have lived in an environment where there were reasons not to trust others. We might then anticipate that people are untrustworthy in general. This generalization will prompt us to suspect rather than trust.

So, how do we conquer the weakness of protective paranoia?

▶ *Avoid extremes.* No matter how deep the pain or how serious the loss, it's not possible that everyone is out to get us. Thinking in extremes will drive our paranoia and produce extreme behavior, such as that we saw in Mack.

▶ *Tell and accept the truth.* We use our perception that everyone is out to get us as motivation to stay on guard. We mistakenly think that it'll keep us from harm. Yet, it won't. We're deluded if we think that we have the power to keep ourselves perfectly safe. What we do have is the ability to keep ourselves responsibly safe, both physically and emotionally.

▶ *Refuse and distract.* Once we've determined the truth of the situation and that protection is not needed, we must refuse to entertain paranoid thoughts, and instead must distract our thoughts elsewhere.

Mack was afraid to trust again. He didn't know how to regain his sense of safety. In the process of trying to protect himself he made the faulty assumption that it was possible to prevent further losses by being on guard. Instead, he fueled his weakness of protective paranoia. When he examined his thinking and his words, he found that he was not living in truth, and he decided to change this. He invested himself in understanding and living in the current truth, and over time he gained strengths in self-discipline, truth, personal responsibility, and forgiveness.

The companion weaknesses that accompany protective paranoia vary. The ones checked here are the most likely companion weaknesses to Mack's paranoia.

Companion Weaknesses

1	6	11√	16√	21√	26√	31	36	41√	46√
2	7	12	17√	22	27√	32√	37	42	47√
3√	8√	13√	18	23	28√	33√	38√	43	48
4√	9	14	19√	24	29	34√	39	44	49√
5	10	15	20	25√	30√	35	40	45	50√

NINE

Excessive Self-Focus

There was a brief time in my life when skiing was the most impor- tant thing of all. I thought about it when I went to sleep. I thought about it when I woke up. If I hadn't known better I would have thought it was a religion. I had to wear certain kinds of clothes, know the best slopes, have the best skis, get there as early as possible, and get just one more run in before the lift closed. It was completely consuming.

Most of us do this at some point in our lives. Some go through the car phase. Some go through the dating phase. Teenagers focus on looks. Young actors are consumed by their craft. All of us focus on our- selves to some degree, and from time to time that focus can be more intense than at other times. If that intense focus on ourselves contin- ues, however, it can become a weakness.

But What About Me?
Weakness: Excessive Self-Focus or Self-Concern

I knew a guy once whose focus in life had a remote control attached to it. You could take a forklift, scoop him up with his whole house, him sitting in the same chair he's been in for the last five thousand years, and as long as you didn't change the TV channel, he'd never know you were there. What's that you say? You know this guy?

This can happen when we become so accustomed to what we have and who we're with that we fade away into accidental indifference. The television becomes the mind-numbing, mood-altering focus. Yet we

193

don't all focus on the TV. Some of us become excessively self-focused.

This may show up in the form of a husband, wife, or friend who seems to enter the course of conversation only when they choose, not so much as a part of the conversation but as one obliged to comment from time to time. The rest of the time they're out there in space somewhere, preoccupied with something they prefer to think about, something that doesn't involve others. This is a person who's there, but not there.

We all have times in our lives when we're this way. It happens when we're working on special projects, or experiencing grief or some other strong emotion. That's normal. Yet, what I'm talking about here is a lifestyle of excessive self-involvement. Someone who becomes removed from others emotionally, psychologically, and spiritually. This isn't healthy. It costs those of us who are self-focused and all of those around us. Brian is an example of this.

Brian

When people met Brian, they were often struck by his genuine interest in them. They could sit and talk with him for hours. He was attentive to their comments, responsive to their emotional cues, reasonably self-disclosing. Just being with him made others feel comfortable and welcome. Yet, this wasn't always the case. In recent years Brian has made some dramatic changes in his life.

When Brian came to me he'd reached the heights of his career and succeeded in every way except in feeling satisfied with what he'd done. He was well traveled, was married with three children, had two homes in beautiful areas of the country, and owned whatever he wanted. Brian attended church regularly and sat on the church board. Yet Brian, having everything, in the long run felt that he had nothing. Nothing satisfied him.

For years Brian had concerned himself with Brian and not much else. People and things were merely acquisitions to him. Service to the church was just an empty obligation. Brian couldn't seem to step outside of himself into anyone else's world. He was trapped inside his own, preoccupied with his growing dissatisfaction with all things. Brian was reaping the rewards of focusing on his wants and needs at the expense of investing in others.

What are the origins of this weakness of excessive self-focus?

Self-absorption. It may be a product of self-absorption, thinking about ourselves all of the time, good old-fashioned selfishness. We're concerned with what we want and how we feel, to the near exclusion of others. It doesn't matter if we damage the family finances, we want this thing and we're going to buy it. It doesn't matter if someone wants our attention, we're reading a book. We're watching our show on TV—don't bother us. On the other hand, we don't care if you're in the middle of a TV show, we demand that you stop and listen to us! This was the case with Brian. Remember, I'm not talking about isolated instances; I'm talking about excessive behavior.

Privileged expectation. We may have been excessively praised or never held accountable. We thus may have been raised to think only of ourselves.

Excessive independence. Excessive self-focus may result from excessive independence. We don't need your help. Sure, come along if you want to, we don't care if you do or don't. We can't be there for dinner with you guys. We're going to the gym or out with our friends.

Dependency. We may also be so focused on our own needs that others' needs don't matter. No! You have to stay home with us. We don't like it when you go out with others. We need you here all of the time.

Traumatic events or environments. We may become self-focused because events or environments have encouraged us to focus on our own survival. We and our survival may remain our focus when we leave that environment.

So, how can we overcome the weakness of excessive self-focus?

▶ *Review.* If possible, find out where this self-focus originated. Does it make sense to continue it? That's how we've been. Is that the way we want to continue to be?

▶ *Force focus.* We need to force ourselves to consider others. Start focusing on others and what they're saying. Try to understand why they think the way they do. We need to starve our weakness of excessive self-focus by forcing ourselves to develop interest in others. This will leave us with very little energy to focus on ourselves.

▶ *Resist.* We must resist the urge to excessively focus on ourselves. When the urge hits us, we should immediately distract our thoughts to an interest in something or someone else.

▶ *Release.* We need to release those whom we have captured for our own purposes. We should become concerned more with their welfare and their interests than with our selfish interests in them.

What Brian was experiencing was the inevitable result of caving in to the weakness of self-focus. Too much self-focus is terribly unhealthy. We're made to share. We're social creatures. If we become isolated within ourselves, we eventually emotionally disintegrate. The very definition of madness may be hidden in excessive self-focus. Brian used what was fueling his weakness to instead develop the strengths of love, sacrifice, compassion, service, relationship, and humility.

Companion Weaknesses

1	6√	11√	16	21√	26	31	36	41	46√
2√	7	12	17	22	27	32	37	42√	47√
3√	8√	13√	18	23	28	33√	38√	43	48√
4	9	14	19	24√	29	34	39	44	49√
5	10	15√	20	25	30√	35	40	45	50√

I Don't Care What You Think
Weakness: Insensitivity

Do you have a period of time in your life that you'd like to erase? I have several, one of them coming to mind as I write. In my twenties I went through a period when I mistakenly thought I knew everything and was sure I needed to say it. I had confused honesty with obnoxiousness, and was unable to recognize what I was doing. If there had been such a thing as an insensitivity meter, I'm sure my attitude and remarks would have thrown it off the chart. During that time I really didn't care what others thought. Moreover, I saw myself as exceptionally brave and authentic. Meantime, I was hurting myself and lots of other people. I thank God for all of the hard knocks that came my way as a result of all of that foolish thinking and behavior. I don't want to ever be so self-deceived again.

Rita is another example of the weakness of insensitivity, and most of us have known someone like her.

Rita
Rita was the director of a rather large department within a larger company. She was extremely successful at her job but the turnover rate in her department was alarming. The reasons for this weren't hard to discern. All I had to do was listen to the way she'd talk to people: "That was a stupid thing to do!" she'd say. "What made you think you could do it that way? You don't have a clue!"

To Rita, people were important only if she could use them in some way. If their function was no longer necessary, they were expendable. Those who worked with her lived in dread that they might cross her path on the wrong day and be swiftly dismissed from planet workplace.

What are the origins of the weakness of insensitivity?

Modeled behavior. A look at Rita's background sheds ample light on her behavior. Rita's mother was extremely controlling and demeaning. Her father was passive and compliant. Rita thus had two models of behavior. One she subscribed to for herself and the other provided what she expected from those around her.

Insecurity. Some of us are insensitive because we can't tolerate criticism. We shut people off to avoid hearing their complaints. We also convince ourselves that we don't need other people. That way they can't hurt us. At that point we don't care what they think. Like those around Rita, they become expendable.

Privileged expectation. Some of us have been raised without having been taught to consider others, or we have, along the way, come to believe that we're better than others. We can't let others know this, so we pretend to be accepting, and then in moments of frustration or anger our underlying disdain comes out in the form of insensitivity.

How can the weakness of insensitivity be overcome?

▶ *Recognize and admit our insensitivity.* We won't change what we can't see or won't admit. People might not always be willing to tell us about our insensitivity, so we must be alert to their responses to us. Are we hurting their feelings? Do they go silent when we talk to them or criticize them? We need to ask them if we seem insensitive to them. Then we must take responsibility for the harm we've done and seek to restore relationships.

▶ *Determine the origin of the insensitivity.* Where did we learn this type of behavior? Did someone else in the family act this way? Did it bother us? Do we see that this is learned behavior?

▶ *Determine our course of action and act.* Whether we find the source of our insensitivity or not, the issue is still the same. We need to decide who we want to be and determine to move in that direction. If we mentally construct a responsible internal picture of who we want to be and how we want to behave, our insensitive behavior will come up against that picture and become uncomfortable to us.

▶ *Seek accountability.* We need to find others who can hold us accountable for how we treat others.

There's a great verse in the Psalms where King David looks to God for mercy. *"Do not withhold your mercy from me, O Lord; may your love and your truth always protect me"* (Ps 40:11). I think that's an important connection and a sure cure for insensitivity:

Principle: Never separate love and truth. If we do, one becomes a lie and the other a hammer.

Rita had a lot of fences to mend, and it took quite a long time to do it. She had to starve her own self-interest and begin to consider others. When she did, it was her weakness of insensitivity that disintegrated instead of her friendships. She developed strengths in the areas of accurate self-perception, humility, and accountability.

Companion Weaknesses

1	6	11√	16	21√	26	31	36	41√	46√
2	7	12	17√	22√	27	32	37	42	47√
3	8√	13√	18√	23	28	33	38√	43√	48√
4√	9	14	19	24√	29	34	39	44	49√
5	10√	15	20	25	30	35	40	45√	50√

Never Mind the Budget, I'll Buy It Anyway
Weakness: Avoidant Compartmentalizing

Some compartmentalizing is not only good, it's necessary. We leave home behind when we go to work. We're still aware of home and have contact throughout the day, but in the main we're focused on work.

This is a type of compartmentalizing that has easily penetrable walls. It allows us to concentrate more on one thing than another. People who work at home find that without this compartmentalization, work becomes difficult. The same is true of runners who need to focus on a race or drivers who need to focus on the road. Yet, there's a kind of compartmentalizing that isn't healthy, and if repeatedly subscribed to, it will become a weakness. Avoidant compartmentalizing has walls that are less easily penetrated and serve to keep reasonable responsibility out of conscious view.

The weakness of avoidant compartmentalizing can be quite costly. Many men have gotten involved in pornography and affairs by placing those activities into mental and experiential compartments that they choose to experience as detached from the rest of their lives. They do this to avoid any amount of awareness that could keep them from what they're doing. The reality is that the only thing that separates these compartments is denial, waiting to be shattered. Yet this is not the only type of avoidant compartmentalizing. Let me tell you about Clarisse.

Clarisse

Clarisse came to therapy with her husband and at his demand. He complained that she was spending too much money. She shopped excessively even though she'd promised him many times that she wouldn't. Now, the finances were in a state of disaster and her husband was ready to leave her.

Clarisse was spending money and shopping as a way of altering her mood. She was unhappy at home, feeling overwhelmed by life and detached from her husband's emotions. Spending made her feel alive. Clarisse had tried many different methods to stop the spending but she always found a way to continue. Why was that? Clarisse had learned to use the tool of avoidant compartmentalizing. She had separated the world of spending from the world of accountability and that meant that accountability was useless. Why did Clarisse overspend?

For Clarisse, this weakness developed as a response to her low self-esteem. Feeling unimportant, Clarisse would slip into a fantasy world where she'd feel powerful and important. She was escaping her feeling of insignificance. The saleswomen at the stores became her social contacts. Since those relationships would disappear if she didn't maintain them, her spending continued. And to avoid the loss of the only sense of importance Clarisse had, she kept her spending world compartmentalized.

So, where does the weakness of avoidant compartmentalizing originate?

Past trauma. If in our pasts we experienced trauma, we may have taught ourselves to disconnect harmful information from our conscious selves.

Immaturity. Teenagers often have a sense of invincibility. Nothing can happen to them. They see on the news that other teenagers do get hurt, but they avoidantly compartmentalize that information as being about someone else, not themselves.

Fear, avoidance of guilt, and avoidance of responsibility. When we don't want to consider the consequences of something, or if we feel that it will hurt us or someone we love, we may banish it to a mental compartment and disconnect it from the rest of our lives. The partition between this behavior and the rest of our lives is quite thin. We get used to it, and the more success we have with keeping these worlds separate, the more we place our confidence in the fragile partition. Eventually, however, these worlds will collide, and when they do, they'll both fall apart.

So, how do we overcome this weakness?

▶ *Recognize the weakness.* We first need to recognize the weakness. How do we know it's there? Because, in order for us to have pushed this information into a compartment in the first place, we had to have seen it. We deliberately make determinations about what to keep in our conscious thought and what to banish. Every move we make in this regard should reaffirm to us that we're deliberately causing this to happen.

▶ *Tear down the partition.* When there's information that we have the urge to compartmentalize in order to avoid consequences or responsibility, we need to stop ourselves from doing so. We must let the thoughts remain conscious and allow the worlds to collide in our minds. Then we need to deal with the issues instead of running away from them.

▶ *Determine the underlying issues and resolve them.* What are we trying to hide? Why are we trying to hide it? If necessary, we must get help in dealing with these issues.

▶ *Stay exposed.* Never do anything that you're unwilling to have others know about.

▶ *Find accountability.* We shouldn't go this alone. We need to find someone who'll require us to be accountable for our thoughts and behaviors.

Clarisse had quite a difficult time giving up her avoidant compartmentalizing, because shopping had become her world. She had nothing else on which to fall back. However, as she pulled her energies away from shopping and compartmentalizing and invested them in honest disclosure and accountability, she began to change her world. In the long run she developed the strengths of honesty, humility, and self-discipline.

Companion Weaknesses

1√	6√	11√	16	21√	26	31	36	41√	46√
2√	7√	12√	17√	22	27	32√	37	42	47√
3√	8√	13√	18	23	28	33√	38√	43	48√
4√	9	14	19	24√	29	34√	39√	44√	49√
5√	10	15√	20	25	30	35	40√	45	50√

Everybody Is Looking at Me
Weakness: Excessive Self-Awareness

With the exceptions of God's grace and mercy, I find receiving gifts to be one of the most complicated and challenging experiences in life. How can a person look at a boxed gift, all wrapped in beautiful paper, and not get excited about what's inside just for him or her? I don't believe it's possible. So there you are, right in front of the giver with your jaw down to the ground, as eager as a hungry Chihuahua. Can you see how this might present a problem?

Let's say that you were hoping for roller skates (not that this has ever happened to me, of course). You lift up the box, anticipating its weight to be consistent with the weight of roller skates, and you almost send it flying back over your head because it's so light that it's clearly not what you were hoping for. Now what? The only thing you can be is excessively self-aware at that moment. Do you register disappointment or pretend continued excitement? What do you do when you finally open the box and it contains packets of multicolored underwear with the names of the days of the week embroidered on them? Now you're supposed to stand there and genuinely be thrilled. I don't know about you, but for me, this exercise in human development is just too much.

People are sometimes like packages, thinking one thing on the inside and presenting something else on the outside. Unfortunately, excessive self-awareness breeds in these cases. Renae struggled with this weakness.

Renae

On the outside Renae seemed to be extremely competent and capable, as she and her husband served as leaders in a community-based organization. No one but her husband knew that her internal experience was quite different from what she put forward publicly.

Renae invested a great deal of time in being concerned with what other people thought of her and of her husband. This concern drove her behavior, and because she was more concerned with what others thought than with her integrity, she lived in a state of compromise.

She manipulated others in order to meet her goals. She became excessively critical of her husband if he appeared to let their image be diminished. She was so afraid of making mistakes that she was reluctant to take the risks required to meet the goals they held in common. She smiled outwardly only to complain in private. Occasionally her frustration would create a crack in her façade and she'd become pushy and intolerant, unable to hide for just a moment her unrelenting need for approval.

She came to me depressed, complaining of self-dissatisfaction and self-doubt. In reality she was unable to maintain the façade any longer.

"I just don't have the energy anymore," she said.

"To do what?" I asked.

"I can't keep on doing what I'm doing," she said. "I can't continue to keep these people motivated and moving forward with these projects."

"Is the job too much for you?" I asked.

"It shouldn't be," she replied.

"Then let's find out where the energy is going," I suggested.

I listened to Renae as she accounted not only for her time but for many of her thoughts during the course of the previous week. What an amazing person! I could only dream of being able to accomplish in one week what she did. What was more amazing was that she'd done all of that work even though she was mentally and emotionally at war with herself almost the entire time. It was the internal war that was claiming so much of her energy.

Renae was consumed with anxiety brought about by her insecurities. She pummeled herself with doubts about whether she was doing the right thing, and whether others approved. She was so insecure that she couldn't let anyone under her leadership fail because she feared that would negatively reflect upon her. She couldn't let her husband fail, for the same reason. This is what led her into manipulating others and complaining. Trying to manage her insecurities led Renae to develop the weakness of excessive self-awareness. It was a consuming weakness, stealing her life away.

What are the origins of the weakness of excessive self-awareness?

Insecurity, anxiety, and fear. Because Renae's insecurities were never addressed and resolved, she had to invest a great deal of energy in managing them. They were often calling out to her with anxiety or fear. She then had to repress the feelings and act as if they weren't there. Her excessive self-awareness became consuming. Her authenticity was destroyed. The weakness was consuming all available mental and emotional energy. This is why Renae was feeling drained.

Excessive self-focus. The more we focus on ourselves, the more likely we are to become excessively self-aware. Self-focus is literal concentration on ourselves as the topic and main interest of our lives, at the expense of all others. Self-awareness is a condition we may experience as internal indicators make themselves known and require our attention. As an example, a champion chess player may become excessively aware when, in the silence of the game, he hears and feels his heart pounding. Renae's self-awareness was brought about by the internal and subjective experience of feeling anxiety and fear.

How can the weakness of excessive self-awareness be overcome?

▶ *Recognize excessive self-awareness.* Are we anxious or afraid? Are we worried? Are we depressed? Are we angry?

▶ *Resolve any issues that are the focus of excessive self-awareness.* Allow the internal signal to prompt resolution of the underlying issue rather than management of the signal. Otherwise the excessive self-awareness will never go away.

▶ *Turn any excessive internal focus to an outward focus.* Talk about it. Expose it. Don't hold on to it as if it were a treasure. It's a principle: If you want to slay it you have to *say* it! Never make bad things sacred, which is what happens when we hide them in secret.

In facing and dealing with her weakness of excessive self-awareness, Renae won back the energy that had been stolen away. She put it into developing the strengths of reasonable self-examination, reasonable expectations, reasonable personal responsibility, and mercy.

Companion Weaknesses

1√	6√	11√	16√	21√	26√	31√	36√	41	46√
2√	7√	12√	17√	22√	27√	32√	37√	42	47√
3√	8√	13√	18√	23√	28√	33√	38√	43	48√
4√	9√	14√	19√	24√	29	34√	39√	44	49√
5√	10	15√	20√	25√	30√	35√	40√	45√	50√

I Want It Now
Weakness: The Tendency to Be Impulsive or Impatient

I rode a bird dog once, a reddish-brown spotted one. It was a short ride. I was sitting on the steps to the house, minding my own business and then there he was, right in front of me, just staring at me. I was just a little kid, and to me he was about the size of a horse, so I treated him like one. I jumped on his back, put my arms around his neck, and held on for dear life. Roy Rogers would've been proud!

A few seconds later I was reclining on the lawn, staring at the sky, and asking myself what over years became the familiar question of "Why did I do that?" It seems clear to me now that I did it because the dog dared me to do it. Yet, back then, it just seemed automatic. I was responding to an impulse. It wasn't the first time I'd done that, nor would it be the last.

Both impatience and impulsivity are overly concerned with self. Impatience is the more obvious, as it tends to be more aggressive and is often aimed at someone else. Impulsivity can be more subtle.

Certainly it can also be obvious, as with someone who spends the family income on gambling or whatever they desire at the expense of others. Yet let me show you Rhonda, an example of impulsiveness that's more subtly self-focused. In fact, it looks almost the opposite.

Rhonda

"The church office called me last week and asked me to handle the decorations for the Christmas concert. I immediately told them I'd do it, and then I got so mad!" Rhonda said. "I'm always saying yes when I should be saying no. I just can't help myself. I just say yes automatically and hate myself later."

"That's interesting," I said. "You just said no. So, apparently you can say no. You just don't. Why not?"

"Well," Rhonda said, "I don't want to disappoint the church."

"Why not?" I asked again.

"Well," she said, "I don't want to be irresponsible."

"But, what you're saying is that you end up making yourself over-responsible and angry when you say yes," I went on. "Can you see how that can be irresponsible, when it comes to taking proper care of yourself?"

"Yes," she said.

"And then I would imagine that you can't let your anger show, so you pretend to be happy about doing the work."

"That's right," Rhonda said.

"So, actually," I said, "saying yes and not saying no puts you in the position of being irresponsible, over-responsible, and inauthentic."

"I'd never thought of it like that," Rhonda said.

"That's because your thinking has become almost automatic and you're now acting on an impulse."

As Rhonda and I talked, it became clear that Rhonda was afraid of letting the church down, because she didn't want to be rejected. Her overcommittment was actually an avoidant maneuver, avoiding rejection. Yes, she did want to serve the church, and that was a good thing.

Yet, it wasn't a good thing for her to be overcommitting herself and pretending to be serving happily when she actually resented the work.

Rhonda had distanced herself from an awareness of her protective motives by justifying her behavior. Instead of thinking about why she had the urge to say yes, she immediately said yes, telling herself that it was because she wanted to serve. Whenever she felt this urge, her response was to say yes. It had become her automatic response to the urge.

What are the origins of the weaknesses of impulsiveness and impatience?

Overlooking information. Both impulsiveness and impatience occur when information related to the impulsive or impatient urge isn't given proper consideration. Instead we jump from the urge, via justification, straight into action. As an example, Rhonda was asked to serve, knew she didn't want to, and then said yes. She jumped beyond the middle part of this equation without giving it adequate consideration.

Discomfort with anxiety or fear. Some of us respond on impulse or with impatience if we feel the discomfort of anxiety or fear. By acting on impulse what we're actually trying to do is to get the feeling of anxiety or fear to stop. Unfortunately, we're not dealing with the underlying issue, so the anxiety or fear will continue to grow.

No learned delay. We may not have learned to pause before responding in general. This leaves us with no time to consider the negative repercussions of our actions to self or others.

Privileged expectation. Protected from any responsibility, we may not have learned to be concerned for others or with the repercussions of our responses.

How can we overcome impulsiveness or impatience?

▶ *Consider the whole truth.* Before Rhonda could say no, she had to uncover the whole truth about why she said yes.

▶ *Don't act at the point of the urge.* The only way Rhonda could get back to the whole truth was to stop acting at the point of the urge. Remember that the truth of the matter is in between the initial triggering event and the action. It's in the justification. What Rhonda used as a pause button was a simple comment like, "Let me think about that and get back to you."

▶ *Examine the justification.* Next Rhonda had to determine the reasons behind her automatic behavior, starting with the justification. Rhonda justified her action with the incomplete truth that she wanted to serve. She therefore acted on only part of the truth.

▶ *Act on the whole truth.* Acting on only part of the truth, rather than the whole truth, generally leads to living a lie.

▶ *Make a determination.* Determine the risks of all plausible responses. For Rhonda, the alternative behavior was to say no. The risk would've been that she might have been rejected.

▶ *Keep your principles intact.* Always place integrity above the cost of risk. When we do, we'll find that we're better for having done so, and that we can resolve our fears and anxieties if we don't run from them.

Rhonda withdrew her emotional investment from her weaknesses and rerouted it into moving beyond them. In the process she developed strengths in the areas of peace of mind, honesty, authenticity, delegating, accurate self-perception, and reasonable responsibility.

Companion Weaknesses

1√	6√	11√	16√	21√	26√	31	36	41√	46√
2√	7√	12√	17√	22√	27√	32√	37	42√	47√
3√	8√	13√	18√	23√	28√	33√	38√	43√	48√
4√	9√	14√	19√	24	29	34√	39√	44√	49√
5√	10	15√	20	25√	30√	35	40√	45	50√

TEN

Repeated, Replicated, and Compound Weaknesses

Years ago, I was driving with a friend from the West Coast to mid-America. It was late in the evening when we encountered the awesome beauty of the Rocky Mountains. Even in the dark, they were splendid!

The bright headlights set aglow the tall, thick forest as we followed the curves up the steep and winding road. Every so often a scenic overlook or a gap in the forest would open up and reveal the extraordinary elevation to which we had traveled. The night was clear blue and the stars fanned across the sky so brightly it made us envy the old-time cowboys gazing up from their leather saddle pillows.

It was my turn at the wheel and Dan had the job of keeping me awake with his not-so-fascinating chatter. Staying awake was no real problem, as Dan had the annoying habit of expressing his political views, which were diametrically opposed to mine, always sparking lively banter.

We were lost in the beauty of the Rockies and mutual longings to see deer crossing when suddenly everything changed. In a split second, the skies were gone. The road was gone. At fifty miles an hour we were blinded by bright white. We could see no farther than the headlights' immediate reflection splintering off of something bright and shiny flying through the air. We were engulfed in it.

Thoughts went screaming through my mind. Should I pull over? We could go off a cliff! Should I come to a screeching stop? We could be rear-ended by someone else going fifty miles an hour and caught in this same predicament. Should I keep going? I couldn't see the road! We could drive off a cliff! In as much time as it took to make the decision, I had pulled to a stop.

All around us were long, golden, slender rods, glistening, flailing in the air, and consuming all vacant space until the rods began to settle on the car and the ground. The night began to gradually reappear and parts of the road become visible. I moved ahead a bit to get into clear air space and away from being rear-ended, and we both saw what had happened.

In front of us was a long flatbed truck, jackknifed, with loosened hay bales spilling off the side and onto the highway. It was hay that had filled the air. (I bet you thought it was going to be a spaceship!)

It would have been enough to have to deal with the escaping hay bales in the daytime, or while the car was sitting still, but the combination of the dark night, the glare of the headlights, the speed of the car, and the spilled hay all combined to create a potentially fatal situation. It was the kind of situation that makes you glad that there is a sovereign God watching over us.

It's rare in our lives when only one thing is acting upon us. At any point in time we may be reacting to multiple past and current influences. That's how it is with weaknesses.

Haven't I Been Here Before?
Weakness: The Tendency to Repeat Weaknesses

This is how I make cookies:

I take the common ingredients of tollhouse cookies, put them on the kitchen counter, and begin the process. "OK, I'll start with a bunch of flour." Floof, there it is, in a nice big bowl. If it's not enough I can always add more. "OK, now I need some brown sugar." Floof, now there's a bunch of that in the bowl. If it's not enough I can always add more. Are you noticing a trend yet? "OK, now some eggs and some baking soda or baking powder, whatever. I love vanilla, so I'll use lots of that." If it's not enough I can always add more. I'll put some salt in, but I don't know why. Add the sugar, butter, chips, and whatever else has to be in there. If it's not enough I can always add more.

Once I've added just a bit more of all the things I like, I pop them in the oven, and in moments I have before me cookies the size of Oklahoma! I mail them to my friends at the cost of a small fortune and swear that I'll never do that again! Then I forget all about what happened the last time and do it all over again. Somehow, though, I don't think I'm unique in this. Many of us have the tendency to repeat our mistakes.

Have you ever had an experience that seemed familiar even though you just couldn't tap into when you'd had that experience before? This often happens when weaknesses are repeated in relationships. Frequently those in unhealthy relationships ask themselves, "Haven't I been in this relationship before?" as they come to realize that their current relationship bears great similarity to previous relationships they've had.

It may be a relationship where someone won't commit, where someone is emotionally unavailable, where someone is passively aggressive, or any of a dozen other weaknesses. Why does this happen, and what can we do about it? Let's start with some very basic principles.

Principle: When mistakes are made, acknowledge them and seek to understand how they happened.

Principle: Never fail to use the information gleaned from previous failures to keep from doing the same thing again.

Principle: Identify red flags and never ignore or justify them.

Red flags are those things that give us an indication that there is or will be a problem. When we choose repeatedly to ignore the red flags that we've determined have led us into trouble before, we're responsible for developing a weakness of self-inflicted, unnecessary, and unhealthy vulnerability.

Brett is an example of this tendency to repeat weaknesses.

Brett

Brett came to me with complaints about his second marriage. According to Brett, his wife, Grace, is a "control freak." He "can't get a word in edgewise and can't deal with her getting her way all of the time!" He "might as well have stayed married to Jennifer!"

When I asked him to describe Jennifer as compared to Grace, you would have thought they were the same individual. Not surprisingly, Brett also had had a long-term girlfriend prior to his first marriage who bore great similarities to the two women he eventually married.

The similarities themselves aren't so important as the fact that he ended up in these similar relationships. Why did this happen?

Mothers everywhere will be glad to hear that this had nothing to do with Brett's mother! That was a perfectly healthy relationship. This problem started with his first girlfriend, Becky.

Brett was twenty-three and Becky was twenty-two when they began their three-year relationship. A part of why he liked her was that she was independent and self-motivated. He liked that confidence, as he was confident, too. Not long into the relationship, however, Becky began to be a bit demanding and controlling. At first Brett resisted, and then, tired of the arguments, he just caved in and did whatever Becky wanted. At this Becky began to lose respect for Brett and began to treat him even more inappropriately. Eventually she found someone else and left Brett.

Three months after Becky left him, Brett met Jennifer. They struck up a quick relationship. Brett had already learned from Becky that it was futile to argue, so he actually began the relationship with Jennifer by siding with whatever her wishes were. He chose the path of conflict avoidance, so arguments just didn't exist. Unfortunately, though Brett would always outwardly agree with Jennifer, he felt great anger at some of her decisions, which he then hid. He then blamed Jennifer for these decisions, and grew internally cold and unfeeling, all the while acting as if things were fine. Seven years into the marriage, he had an affair. Jennifer was shocked to learn that Brett had been unhappy with her for almost the entire marriage, which to her recollection had been wonderful. Brett blamed her for being controlling even though he'd actually abdicated all control to her.

Fast-forward to my therapy session with Brett and Grace. He was having the same conversation with Grace that he had had with Jennifer four years before. The good news was that this time he was in therapy. And, yes, he and his wife did get their marriage worked out.

What's the reason for the tendency to repeat weakness?

Failure to review mistakes. When we fail to review our mistakes and extract from them the red flags that will alert us to potential dangers, we don't see the dangers and end up making mistakes again.

Here's what they had (and what we have) to do to get rid of self-inflicted weaknesses.

▶ *Accept responsibility.* Upon evaluating our failures, we must be willing to recognize, admit, and take responsibility for our own weaknesses. Brett didn't reasonably evaluate his first failed relationship, or identify its red flags. He therefore went into his second relationship unprepared to properly protect himself. He should've noted from the first failed relationship that he was drawn to strong, independent women only to find that he didn't know how to hold his own with them. He should have noted that his way of dealing with Becky was to compromise both himself and her and then place the blame on her.

Because Brett didn't evaluate his first relationship, he repeated his mistakes. Along the way he developed weaknesses of passive aggression, conflict avoidance, and repeatedly abandoning responsibility.

In therapy we discussed these weaknesses while analyzing all three of Brett's relationships, and Brett recognized that he was repeating his weaknesses in each relationship. He was finally at step one! Though he had spent years blaming others for his behavior and his failures, he was now able to see his part in them and to recognize that he'd taught himself to deal inappropriately with each of these women. That was hard work on his part and on Grace's as she worked through her own shock at his discontent with their marriage. Now that Brett knew that his behavior was learned, he knew he could work to change it.

Principle: We can't change those things for which we won't take responsibility.

▶ *Resist and learn.* We need to resist responding in the old, unhealthy ways and instead learn new methods of response. When Brett had the urge to cave in and just let Grace have her way, he now recognized that he was facing a crossroad. He had the option of repeating behavior that reinforced his weaknesses, or he could instead use that same emotional and mental energy to build a new strength. Brett chose to talk about how he felt and to state his own preferences. He began to develop strengths in the areas of communication and self-exposure. Then Grace had to accept that Brett had preferences and to deal with her own discomforts. They were beginning to have relationship.

Unfortunately, when we turn away from doing wrong things we often fail to see the incredible power that we used in doing those things. We languish without motivation because, compared to the emotional upheavals of doing what is wrong, doing what is right seems mundane. It feels like all of the passion is gone. Yet this is not the case. The passion is not gone. It is lying dormant and unattended, waiting to be attached to the next adventure we choose. The passion that was strong enough to go against what everyone else was telling us to do, against our own instincts, and against our own best interests still resides within us, waiting for the next assignment. Just think of the passion we'll experience when we know that what we're doing is right!

Companion Weaknesses

1√	6	11	16	21√	26√	31	36	41√	46
2√	7√	12√	17	22	27√	32√	37√	42	47√
3√	8	13√	18	23	28√	33√	38√	43	48√
4√	9	14	19	24	29	34	39√	44	49√
5√	10	15√	20	25	30√	35	40	45	50√

This Is the Way I Am Will Always Be
Weakness: Believing Faulty Assumptions

There are many faulty assumptions we may believe about ourselves: that we must be perfect, that we must have everyone's approval, that conflict will destroy us, that we can't withstand rejection. There are also many faulty assumptions we may believe about others: that they should think as we do, that they should do as we say, that we're less than they are, that they're less than we are, that they'll all abandon us, that they must perceive us accurately, that they don't have weaknesses like we do. I could go on, but far too many trees would have to give up their lives for even an abridged version of all of the faulty assumptions we believe! There's one on which I do want to comment, however. It's an assumption about change.

Nothing stays the same. I suppose Mt. Rushmore might have thought it would remain as it had been for ages, just a mountain of rock in the Black Hills of South Dakota. Yet, along came Gutzon Borglum, who turned it into Washington, Jefferson, Roosevelt, and Lincoln. Just think, if Warner Brothers had gotten there first it might have become Wile E. Coyote, Marvin the Martian, Sylvester, and Tweety Bird!

Even if the mountain had remained untouched by Borglum, however, it still would have gone through changes. Wind, rain, fire, tourists—all of them have affected Mt. Rushmore.

It's the very nature of things and of people to change. That's why I'm always a bit amazed to hear someone say "People never change" or "This is the way I am and this is the way I will always be." Both assumptions are utterly false and ever so common. Jake was an example of this.

Jake

Jake was an extraordinary artist. His friends and family formed a protective circle around him, making excuses for his bad temper and explaining it away. They said that he had a particular type of temperament and that this type of behavior was to be expected from this artistic type. If he yelled at them or demeaned them, they just shared a knowing look with one another as if to say, "Oh well, he's got that artistic temperament."

Every bad behavior that Jake displayed was tolerated for one of three reasons. First, Jake brought in a substantial income, and those around him were dependent upon that income. They also, by association, shared in his celebrity. They further believed, as Jake did, that his was a certain unchangeable personality type, and that therefore the negative behaviors emanating from that personality type should be tolerated. For these reasons, no one would call Jake into any accountability.

Not only did these people feel that Jake had a certain unchangeable type of personality; they subscribed to the same theory regarding themselves. They saw themselves as having certain unchangeable personalities, too. As an example, some of Jake's family and friends saw themselves as having a laid-back personality style. Because of this assumption they excused their failure to call Jake into account. Laid-back or passive personality types just didn't do that kind of thing.

Where does this weakness of belief in faulty assumptions originate?

Endorsement. We may mistakenly assume that something is true because someone we trust has said it is. We may have read books or listened to speakers or friends who've suggested that certain changeable things about us are unalterable.

Misinterpretation. We may have misinterpreted accurate information.

Self-delusion. We may want so badly to believe the false information that we simply convince ourselves that it's true.

Failure to question the truth of what we think. In the long run, the main reason we believe faulty assumptions is because we fail to challenge what is said. We just accept it as truth.

So, how can we overcome a belief in faulty assumptions?

▶ *Question.* It's important for us to question what's said. I'm not suggesting that we stand up in the middle of someone's presentation and challenge him or her. What I'm suggesting is that we consider the things that are being said and make determinations about them. If it's something that demeans or diminishes anyone, absolves us of personal responsibility, or excuses inappropriate thinking and behavior, we need to question it. Maybe we've heard it wrong. If so, we need to seek clarity. Maybe we've heard it right, but it's wrong, and we need to reject it.

▶ *Demand the whole truth.* The whole truth is always the key ingredient. It's not a mystery. Think about our example. "This is the way I am. This is the way I'll always be." There is some truth in this. If we were born in New York, we will always be from New York. In that sense, we will always be the same. Yet, that's only part of the truth. What about the rest of it? The truth is that we can and do change. The issue is that there may be things about us that we either don't want to change or we don't want to invest the energy in changing.

▶ *Admit the whole truth.* Jake had been told for most of his life that he was special. He had been told that he was different in an artistic, creative way, and that it made sense for him to act out as he did. He had been told that it was a part of his artistic temperament and his artistic process. Jake accepted this about himself, and it became the excuse for his bad behavior. People actually gave him encouragement and empathy when they should've been calling him into account for his behavior. If anyone outside of his inner circle ever criticized him, it was attributed to jealousy. Jake had become insulated from the truth and from the growth that rightfully belonged to him, and while others contributed to this situation, in the end Jake was fully responsible for his own predicament.

The road Jake had to travel to healing was a difficult one. He'd had an affair, and that's what landed him in therapy. Someone had finally objected to his behavior. His wife had tolerated everything except this. So much for "Oh, that's his artistic temperament!" The truth is that everyone around Jake had something to gain by tolerating his behavior. Once he violated one of those individuals, however, the whole charade began to fall apart. Everyone started questioning what was going on and why. They should've asked these questions a long time before.

Jake's world was turned upside down. What others had said was acceptable in his behavior was no longer acceptable. He'd known for a long time that he was wrong, and now he had to face it as reality. Interestingly enough, those who had once said that his behavior was a result of his unchangeable temperament were now demanding that he change. Welcome to the weakness of believing faulty assumptions.

Yet, even more powerful than Jake's weakness of believing faulty assumptions was his choice to eliminate it. Jake is still an artist, but he's not misbehaving anymore. He came out of his delusional state and fought like a tiger to straighten himself out. He's another example that God provides grace to people when they need it. In the course of converting his weaknesses to strengths, Jake developed strengths in the areas of truth, honesty, forgiveness, mercy, self-respect and respect of others, courage, responsibility, accurate self-perception, and spiritual development.

Companion Weaknesses

1√	6	11	16	21	26	31	36	41	46√
2√	7	12	17	22	27	32	37√	42	47
3√	8√	13√	18	23	28	33	38√	43	48√
4√	9	14	19	24	29	34	39	44	49√
5	10	15	20	25	30	35	40	45	50√

I Swore I'd Never Be Like This!
Weakness: The Tendency to Replicate Thoughts and Behaviors

I was born in North Carolina, and while I didn't spend a lifetime there, I was there long enough to acquire the accent. It's actually quite a lovely accent, but I found that it drew comments when I was living in other states. I worked hard to eliminate the accent so I didn't have to explain so often where I was from.

On occasion, I have clients who are from my home state. I love the accent on them but, like the flu, I don't want to catch it. The experience, however, is much like a tiny little iron shaving straining to resist a ten-ton magnet. It's futile! Before the session is half over, I sound as if I'd never left North Carolina.

It's amazing just how strong the power of consistent modeling is. It creates for us a type of familiarity that feels somehow like home. It creates in us a type of groove like that of deep tire tracks in an old muddy road. The groove is so powerful that it constrains us and holds us within its power.

Extracting ourselves from the muddy road is easier to accomplish than exiting emotional or behavioral grooves, however, because those grooves are less obvious and more complicated. It's because of these internal grooves that we find ourselves doing what we swore we'd never do and being what we swore we'd never be. Janice and David are good examples here.

Janice and David

Janice and David had struggled for most of their married life with her anger and what she called "his lack of communication." Whenever David would disagree with Janice, she'd become defensive and react angrily. After numerous unsuccessful attempts to "get through" to her, David began to withdraw.

"What's the use?" he would ask. "You don't want to hear what I have to say."

"Yes, I do," she'd reply, "but all you ever do is attack me!"

Over time, any and all serious topics became off limits to Janice and David. Their relationship took on a shallow quality. There were no discussions of depth. There no longer were fights, but there was also no depth of relationship. Their marriage became a sterile, silently painful, parallel existence.

They came to me complaining that they were more like roommates than husband and wife. That had become unacceptable to David. Janice had come to treatment against her wishes. She was content with things just as they were.

Janice had settled for survival. She found substantial comfort in taking the path of least resistance. By subscribing to mutual disengagement in her marriage, Janice would never have to understand herself. She'd never have to explore why she was so defensive and angry. She'd never have to grow in these areas, never come to victory and life in these areas. She'd chosen to survive at a level of lesser pain. She'd seen and done this before.

Janice had grown up with an angry, argumentative father and a mother who never won an argument.

"Dad was always right," Janice explained.

"So, what did that feel like?" I asked.

"It hurt a lot," she said, "and it made me angry!"

"So, what did you do with your anger?" I asked. "Did you sit your dad down and express your discontent with the way he was treating you?"

"No," she said. "I was just a kid. I couldn't sit my dad down and talk to him. He scared me. So, I just stuffed it!"

As a child, Janice experienced a good deal of internal pain from having her opinions negated. She didn't speak out against her father because she was just a child. She was helpless, unable to find resolution. In order to emotionally survive the relationship, she "stuffed" her anger, and now it was coming out at her husband whenever he disagreed with her. She couldn't take any more pain from being invalidated.

Her marriage was suffering from her current behavior related to her childhood pain. To protect herself from any more pain, Janice would strike out in anger. Now, in this particular behavior, she'd become like her father. She'd become a part of all that she'd sworn she'd never be.

Her marriage was slowly dying because Janice had chosen survival instead of life. Once she became willing to settle for nothing less than a life of success, Janice set foot on the path to turning her life and her marriage around.

What are the origins of this weakness of replicating thoughts and behaviors?

Role-modeling and sanctions. Replicated thoughts and behavior frequently develop over time, through role-modeling. As we watch others and listen to how they think, those thoughts and behaviors are sanctioned in our minds. Because the people around us are thinking and behaving in these ways, we reason that it must be OK for us to think and act that way as well.

We may follow the modeling of our parents. They work hard, so it's OK for us also to work hard. They drink excessively, so it's OK for us to do that, too. They yell at each other, so it must be OK for us to yell at each other.

We may follow the modeling of our peers or siblings. They wear blue jeans, so it must be OK for us to wear blue jeans. They own BMWs, so it must be OK for us to own BMWs. They hit us, so it must be OK for us to hit others or for others to hit us.

If we really want to see the power of role-modeling, all we need to do is look at what the entertainment industry has sanctioned and see how it has impacted our culture.

A parent who's frequently angry will sanction that behavior as an acceptable means of communication within the family. Children who are subjected to such modeling may automatically turn to such behavior in their own families and relationships.

The power of sanctioned behaviors may be seen from generation to generation. In the Old Testament, the patriarch Abram lied under pressure, as did his wife, his son, his son's wife, and so on. King David struggled with sexual sin, as did his son.

History. Replicated thoughts and behaviors may be our own past thoughts and behaviors. Some of those replicated thoughts and behaviors may be consistent with current truth and good. We may continue to think as we did in our childhoods that our parents love us or that we like ice cream. The problem arises when replicated thoughts and behaviors from the past are no longer true in our current situation.

When I was a child I thought it was reasonable for me to use my spring-loaded pogo stick as my primary means of transportation. That worked quite well back when I was a child. I doubt, however, that replicating that thinking and behavior would be reasonable today.

The same thing would hold true if today I saw myself as being as helpless as I genuinely was as a child. I'm not helpless today as I was as a child. Hopefully, I'm also not uninformed as I was as a child. It's important to live according to today's truths.

How, then, can we overcome the weakness of replicated thoughts and behaviors?

▶ *Recognize faulty reasoning and make it conform to the truth.* Janice, as a child, was truly helpless in her ability to deal successfully with her dad, but she transferred that helplessness into her relationship with her husband. She was living as if she were helpless to resolve anything in her relationship with her husband. Janice was replicating behavior she'd learned in childhood.

The truth was that Janice was no longer helpless. Further truth was that Janice had learned how to stuff her anger at the expense of learning how to use it to achieve resolution. What she was dealing with now was both replicated behavior and a skills deficit. She had to come to an understanding that she was no longer helpless to deal with her anger properly. She also had to learn how to gain resolution through her anger, rather than stuffing it.

▶ *Relegate old thinking to history.* We do this by replacing old thinking and behavior with new thinking and behavior. We push the old behavior into the past, where it belongs.

Janice reminded herself that she was no longer powerless, as she had been as a child. Instead of thinking of herself as helpless, she determined to learn new ways of resolving conflict. Janice learned that when her husband disagreed with her, this didn't mean she was being negated. It meant that he disagreed with her opinion. He was rejecting her opinion, not her. When she understood that, Janice could listen to David's disagreements without becoming defensive.

Janice practiced these new thoughts and behaviors until they became second nature to her and as automatic as stuffing her anger had been. The same energy that had been used to stuff anger and fuel resentment was instead turned into the strengths of self-awareness, personal responsibility, listening without defense, and creating a much healthier marriage.

Companion Weaknesses

1	6√	1N	16	21	26	31	36	41	46
2	7N	12	1N	22N	27	32	37	42	47
3	8√	13√	18	23√	28	33	38	43	48
4	9N	14	19	24√	29	34	39	44	49N
5	10	15√	20	25√	30	35	40	45	50N

There's No Resolution!
Weakness: The Tendency Toward Mutually Reactive Weaknesses

If we needed someone to applaud us, would we hire a one-handed person and then be surprised and disappointed that they couldn't do it? Of course not! Yet we enter relationships with people, all of whom have weaknesses, and then are surprised and disappointed to find that they have them. Why is that? Why are we surprised to discover that someone has a weakness?

It's because we generally don't admit either our own weaknesses or those of others. We call them something else, perhaps personality traits, or we explain them away with the notion that we or others were simply having a bad day. Without knowing it, we make excuses for ourselves and others, and the weaknesses live on, growing ever more entrenched in our thinking and behavior. The end result is individuals reacting to one another's multiple weaknesses without understanding that that's what they're dealing with. Being unaware that the weaknesses are the culprits, we think that we're the problem. We can't achieve resolution if we don't see the real problem.

Do you remember, in the earliest years of school, how we had two lists on a sheet of paper? One side was a list of pictures and the other was a list of words. The assignment was to draw a line from the picture on one side to the matching word on the other side. I loved that assignment, although I remember having to erase a lot.

Let's use that same format, with a couple of changes. First, instead of words and pictures, let's make one list that corresponds to the weaknesses of one person and another list that corresponds to the weaknesses of another person. Let's make the people friends. The list might look like this:

Jane	**Nancy**
Perfectionistic	Withdraws during conflict

The assignment is then to draw a line from the weakness in one person's list to any weakness in the other person's list that would produce any sort of reaction. With Jane and Nancy, we would draw a line from perfectionist to withdraws during conflict, because those two weaknesses would play upon one another.

Jane's perfectionism would place demands on Nancy, who would withdraw to avoid conflict. Nancy's tendency to withdraw during conflict would aggravate Jane's perfectionism. These two things alone would make it very difficult for Jane and Nancy to ever resolve any kind of conflict. This, of course, would be sufficient to create an unhealthy relationship. So the diagram would show mutual reactions to each others' weaknesses and look like this:

Jane	**Nancy**
Perfectionistic ◄————————►	Withdraws during conflict

Weaknesses, however, never travel alone. Where we find one weakness we'll find another. So, let's look at the lists of weaknesses for Jane and Nancy from a more comprehensive viewpoint. They might look like this:

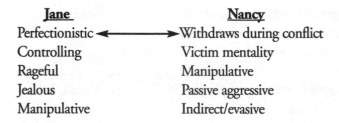

Jane	Nancy
Perfectionistic ⟷	Withdraws during conflict
Controlling	Victim mentality
Rageful	Manipulative
Jealous	Passive aggressive
Manipulative	Indirect/evasive

Jane's controlling behavior would elicit from Nancy her tendency to withdraw during conflict, her tendency to think like a victim, her tendency to manipulate, her passive aggression, and her tendency to be indirect and evasive. Furthermore, all of those weaknesses would spark Jane's tendency to be controlling.

In like manner, most of their weaknesses would play upon one another, causing one reaction after another. At some point the numerous reactions might resemble the splitting of atoms in a nuclear reaction. The mutual reactions of these compound weaknesses would lead to one explosion after another. Our diagram might look something like this:

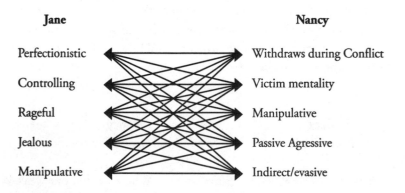

The point here is that no one has just one weakness with which they must contend. When we enter relationship, our weaknesses play upon

the weaknesses of the other person. That's why it's important for us to recognize not only our own weaknesses but also the weaknesses of others.

In fact, I suggest that you make a list of your own weaknesses and of the weaknesses of those with whom you're in relationship. It might help explain why there's so much discord.

Where does this tendency for mutually reactive weaknesses have its origin?

Individual weaknesses coming together in relationship. Remember that each of us has weaknesses that we bring into our relationships. They're there before the relationship begins.

Individual weaknesses developing in response to relationship. We may also develop weaknesses in response to those we encounter within a relationship. As an example, we may not ever have lied before, yet, in a controlling relationship we may feel justified in concealing facts in order to avoid repercussions.

So, how can we overcome the problem of mutually reactive weaknesses?

▶ *Admit and take responsibility for our weaknesses.* Whether they were there before the relationship began or not, these weaknesses are our own individual responsibilities. Unless we admit to and take responsibility for them, we won't be able to change them.

▶ *Lovingly bring the weaknesses of those we love to their attention.* If we genuinely care about others, their weaknesses will be important to us as well. If we love other people, we'll bring their weaknesses to their attention as an act of responsible love. It's not an act of love to overlook someone's weaknesses. It's an act of abandonment and disregard.

▶ *Agree to work on our weaknesses together.* We must agree to be accountable to one another. We need to talk about how we're doing in our quest to eliminate our weaknesses, and we need to let each other know when we see weaknesses reoccurring.

▸ *Divide and conquer.* Each individual in the relationship should deal with his or her own weaknesses. Each weakness needs to be dealt with individually.

▸ *Mutual encouragement.* It's important that we remember to congratulate each other on the changes we're seeing.

Companion Weaknesses

1√	6√	11√	16√	21√	26√	31√	36√	41√	46√
2√	7√	12√	17√	22√	27√	32√	37√	42√	47√
3√	8√	13√	18√	23√	28√	33√	38√	43√	48√
4√	9√	14√	19√	24√	29√	34√	39√	44√	49√
5√	10√	15√	20√	25√	30√	35√	40√	45√	50√

All Messed Up!
Weakness: Compound or Multiple Weaknesses

Let's say that we were born and raised for some eighteen years in an anti-gravity town where water seemed to flow uphill and the furniture seemed to stick sideways to the walls. Our bodies would accommodate the slant in order to keep us upright, so we would learn to walk and stand and even sit at a twenty-degree angle.

Let's say, too, that in this town there was a rule saying that on Mondays, Tuesdays, and all holidays and days of worship, people could make only left-hand turns when driving. Like everyone else in the town, we would endeavor to keep the rules.

Let's say that in addition to those fine features of our existence in our hometown, there were two more such oddities. One was that a comment of "Hello," no matter the context, must be answered with a firm punch in the nose. The other would be that each individual must keep his and his adjacent neighbors' dwellings on all sides painted in an orange and purple plaid.

Then, let's say we moved to New York City, or to Los Angeles, Dallas, or Denver, where none of these attributes exist.

Do you think, having come from the anti-gravity town, that we would feel strange and somehow uncomfortable in our new place? Do you think we'd struggle with feeling that we just didn't belong there? Certainly we would, and that's what life is like for those of us with compound weaknesses. Cindy is a good example.

Cindy

"I feel like I'm going to cry," Cindy said, "but tears don't come. It's a mixture of anxiety and a kind of soft, uneasy, pervasive dread. When I try to put my finger on it, it moves away, just out of reach. But it isn't leaving. I feel desperate."

"What are you thinking?" I asked, trying to get Cindy to identify the thoughts behind the feelings.

"What does she want to talk to me about?" she said. There was a silence after Cindy spoke and a pained look on her face.

I pursued. "What else? What else are you thinking?"

"That's all," she said, "just what does she want to talk to me about?"

"That's not it, Cindy," I went on. "That simple thought, 'What does she want to talk to me about?' would not generate the feelings you're having, or the heightened degree of those feelings. This tells me that there's something else going on in your mind. Go behind the surface thought. What are you thinking? What are you thinking *about* why she might be calling?"

The expression on Cindy's face went from anxiety to intense worry and pain. "I must have done something wrong," she said, wringing her hands.

"What made you think that?" I asked, hoping to get her to look deeper.

"Because, she said she wanted to talk to me when we got a chance," Cindy went on. "Why would she have said it that way if she wasn't going to tell me something bad?"

I noticed Cindy's expression move from worry to fear. I quickly went on with the questioning so we wouldn't lose these fleeting thoughts. "Where's your mind going? What thoughts are you locking onto?"

"I wonder if it was something I said to her last night," she thought out loud. "I wonder if Bob knows anything about it? I wonder if she's talked to him about it? But why would she have to wait to tell me? I wonder how long she's wanted to say something? Maybe she's been wanting to tell me for some time. Maybe I should call her. Maybe I should arrange to meet with her right away. I hate this. I feel so sick. I hate it when someone tells me that they want to tell me something. I always wonder what I did wrong! I always think it's me!"

To some people, drinking may be an area of weakness. Others may suffer from a physical weakness. Some may struggle with a weak faith. Cindy's weaknesses had to do with a crisis orientation, extreme thinking and behavior, faulty assumptions, being guilt-prone, and having a condemning conscience, to name a few.

For some reason Cindy tended to fill in the blanks with the worst-case scenario. This was a pattern in her life, not a onetime experience. It was something she struggled with frequently, and it negatively affected her life and relationships. At times it dominated her life.

Yet much of what Cindy struggled with had no name, and no formal treatment methodology devised for it. So, Cindy didn't call it anything. She just continued, until our sessions, to live with its byproducts of anxiety and self-doubt. That's what happens when we can't identify our problems. We can't change what we can't or won't see.

I continued the session with Cindy. "You said this isn't the first time you've felt this way."

"No," she went on. "Whenever I don't know what someone is thinking, I wonder if they're thinking something bad about me. I always wonder if I've done something wrong."

"Why do you do that?" I asked. "When you have a choice to think a number of different things, why do you choose the assumption that you're at fault? Why do you fill in the blanks with anything at all?"

"I don't know," Cindy said. "I've always done that."

"Is it OK with you that you do something without knowing why you do it?" I asked.

"No," she said. "I guess I just didn't realize I was doing it."

"Well," I said, "you seem to be struggling with weaknesses in a number of different areas. Your struggles with these weaknesses are contributing to your anxiety and depression. If you're willing to look at these weaknesses, and their effects on your life, you can do something about them." Cindy agreed, and over the course of therapy she began to understand what her weaknesses were, where they came from, and how to deal with them.

Cindy had been raised by a father who was not skilled at encouraging children. He was absorbed in his work and with the loss of his wife to cancer when Cindy was two years old. In his grief, he withdrew into himself. In this way Cindy's father unintentionally abandoned her. That abandonment left Cindy with fears of rejection and abandonment. As a way of prohibiting any further abandonment, Cindy learned to do what she could to please her father and avoid rocking the boat. This became the basis for Cindy's performance orientation, people pleasing, and conflict avoidance. Because of that chronic concern for keeping her relationship with her father stable, Cindy began to take her cues for how she was to be from him rather than from herself. She began to rely more on what she perceived in his face and behavior than on what she thought of herself. This led Cindy to become dependent on others for her own self-definition and to base her self-worth on others' opinions.

Certainly, we all care about what others think, but we're not willing to be defined by them. Cindy, having based her self-worth on what others thought of her, now lived with the fluctuation of her self-worth based upon their opinion. Her self-worth was now dependent on others. Her moods shifted with their fluctuating appraisals.

The loss of her mother and the emotional inability of her father to give her the approval she needed as a child further reinforced Cindy's people-pleasing behavior. This time the objective of the people pleasing was not so much protection from rejection as the acquisition of approval. This encouraged in Cindy the development of approval-seeking behavior and reinforced her performance orientation.

For Cindy's father, his two daughters were constant reminders of his loss, and he used anger to keep them at a distance. The less he saw of them, the less grief he felt. Cindy was just a child. She couldn't comprehend his loss and she thought that she'd done something wrong and that this was why her father was so angry with her.

"Get out of here!" he would yell. "Can't you see I just need to be alone? Can't you see you're in my way?"

Cindy tried to read her dad's mind. She tried to see what he said she should see. Yet what she was looking for was what she'd done wrong. Cindy carried that behavior into adulthood, trying to read the minds of others, to fill in the blanks, and when she did, she was still looking for what she had done wrong. She now had a negative bias from which to view herself. She had become uncomfortable with ambiguity. She always wanted to know what people were thinking, because that way she had no blanks to fill in. She had learned to find her security in information. This chronic dependency on the information of others led Cindy to a life of high anxiety.

There is so much more to the story and to the development of her weaknesses, but her story has done what I wanted it to do here. Like Cindy, we all have multiple weaknesses, and we're all affected by the weaknesses of others.

Once Cindy understood when and how her thinking and behavior had developed the way it did, she was ready to make changes. Cindy came to me because of her difficulty with self-doubt, but as you can see, there were many tentacles to that self-doubt, many companion weaknesses.

Cindy had to identify, understand, and deal with each and every one of her weaknesses, not just the obvious few. She learned so much from dealing with her weaknesses that eventually, the sight of a weakness became a signal, indicating to her that she was about to learn and grow. She developed too many strengths to mention here. The reality is that the more weaknesses we have to deal with, the more strength we'll develop.

Companion Weaknesses

1√	6√	11√	16√	21√	26√	31√	36√	41√	46√
2√	7√	12√	17√	22√	27√	32√	37√	42√	47√
3√	8√	13√	18√	23√	28√	33√	38√	43√	48√
4√	9√	14√	19√	24√	29√	34√	39√	44√	49√
5√	10√	15√	20√	25√	30√	35√	40√	45√	50√

Conclusion

It's Quite Simple, Really

Elijah was afraid and ran for his life. When he came to Beersheba in Judah, he left his servant there, while he himself went a day's journey into the desert. He came to a broom tree, sat down under it, and prayed that he might die. "I have had enough, Lord," he said. "Take my life; I am no better than my ancestors." Then he lay down under the tree and fell asleep. All at once an angel touched him and said, "Get up and eat."

1 KINGS 19:3-5

Elijah was having a bad day and got all depressed. Boy, have I been there! I'll bet some of you have, too. This story is such an incredible comfort to me. It makes me thankful for my limitations.

If we climb a tall mountain without stopping to rest, at some point we'll run out of energy. As with Elijah, our human energies are limited. That's a good thing. Let me tell you why.

To accomplish one thing, we must draw our energies away from other things. We have to do that because our God-given energies are limited. Strangely enough, that almost ensures our success. If we invest our emotional, psychological, physical, and spiritual energies in transforming our weaknesses into strengths, success is virtually unavoidable. If we invest those same energies in maintaining our weaknesses, failure is unavoidable. It's that simple.

Somehow we know that. It's like an open secret. We tell our children to turn off the TV and do their homework. Why? It's because we have only so much energy, and watching TV will siphon off some of that energy from homework. Should that continue, the inevitable result will be failure.

Principle: The distance between success and failure is the width of the will. It's one simple, repetitive choice about where we direct our energies.

It's not about the amount of energy invested. That's one reason why some of us don't work toward success. We mistakenly think success requires more effort and energy than failure, that weakness takes less energy than strength. Yet that's not true. Just think of the amount of energy required to avoid responsibility, feel guilty about it, and recover from the repercussions of it. Failure and weaknesses are consuming. We're going to be investing our energies somewhere, no matter what. The difference between failure and success isn't in the amount of energy invested; it's in the object of the investment. What is our focus?

If Elijah had invested his energies in trusting God, he would have robbed his negative, fearful thinking of its ability to exist. It's very much an either/or situation. In the first part of this book, we looked at a passage from Deuteronomy where God set a choice before the people. He said that the choice was between life and death and then he told them (and us) to choose life. Again, it was an either/or situation. When we choose to understand and deal with our weaknesses, we're doing so with the very fuel we previously used to maintain them. We are using the very substance of weaknesses to transform them into strengths.

Principle: Our insecurities, our fears, are there to serve us, not the other way around. When they surface, it means that we've just been given another area from which we may draw fuel for strength and success.

We must remember that failure and weakness are as much choices as strength and success. None of them just happen. We make them happen.

Our limitations, like Elijah's, are blessings in disguise. They force us into choice. We can only do so much. For this reason, our weaknesses force us to evaluate the quality of our lives. They force us to consider whether we are living our lives according to weaknesses or strengths. They make us aware that we are responsible for our lives and our choices.

One thing is certain. Our weaknesses will remain and will continue to rob us of strength unless we dismantle them and use their materials to build something else. In the account of Elijah, in the midst of his pain, God sent him food and rest to strengthen him, and truth to encourage him. Elijah eventually withdrew his energies from his fears and invested instead in God's plan. His strength returned.

It's my hope that *Winning Over Weaknesses* has provided you with a blueprint, a manual for turning your weaknesses into strengths. Perhaps now, when an insecurity strikes or anger appears, you'll be prompted to challenge the weakness and extract from it the fuel that rightfully belongs to your strength and success in life. Perhaps it's one of the greatest secrets in life that understanding and transforming our weaknesses is the key to a life of strength, success, and even greatness.

Companion Weaknesses

1. Fears of rejection or abandonment
2. Fear of intimacy
3. Fear of loss
4. Fears of potential harm
5. Fear of failure or success
6. Performance orientation
7. Conflict avoidance
8. Perfectionism
9. Crisis orientation
10. Discomfort with emotional expression
11. Needing to be right
12. Need for approval
13. Being controlling
14. Self-doubt
15. Not taking responsibility
16. Extreme responses to something unfair
17. Quickness to anger
18. Extreme or unnegotiated expectations
19. Excessive need to be seen accurately
20. Self-loathing
21. Mistaken self-perception
22. Excessive self-reliance
23. Being over-responsible
24. Disregard of others
25. Demanding agreement
26. Extreme thinking
27. Extreme behaviors
28. Emotional reactivity
29. Lack of integration
30. Isolation or dependency
31. Being defined by others
32. Moodiness
33. Depression
34. Personalizing
35. Condemning conscience
36. Discomfort with compliments
37. Misunderstanding personal differences
38. Distorted perceptions
39. Fear of exposure
40. Protective paranoia
41. Excessive self-focus
42. Insensitivity
43. Avoidant compartmentalizing
44. Excessive self-awareness
45. Impulsivity or impatience
46. Repeating weaknesses
47. Faulty assumptions
48. Replicating behaviors
49. Mutual reactive weaknesses
50. Compound weaknesses